THE QUALITY LIBRARY

A Guide to Staff-Driven Imp
Better Efficiency, and Happier

Sara Laughlin and Ray W. Wilson

American Library Association
Chicago   2008

Composed by ALA Editions with typefaces Garamond and Avant Garde Gothic using InDesign 3.0 on a PC platform.

The paper used in this publication meets the minimum requirements of American National Standard for Information Sciences—Permanence of Paper for Printed Library Materials, ANSI Z39.48-1992. ∞

Library of Congress Cataloging-in-Publication Data
Laughlin, Sara, 1949–
    The quality library : a guide to staff-driven improvement, better efficiency, and happier customers / Sara Laughlin and Ray W. Wilson.
        p.   cm.
        Includes bibliographical references and index.
        ISBN 978-0-8389-0952-2 (alk. paper)
        1. Library administration—United States. 2. Total quality management—United States. 3. Library planning—United States. 4. Customer services—United States.
    I. Wilson, Ray W. II. Title.
        Z678.L345 2008
        025.1—dc22   2007030710

ISBN-13: 978-0-8389-0952-2
ISBN-10: 0-8389-0952-3

Printed in the United States of America

12   11   10   09   08   5   4   3   2   1

Contents

Foreword

The books keep coming back. The circulation staff members check them in. The books pile up on the book trucks with an unsorted label. Then gridlock—the trucks congregate in an open area just beyond the circulation desk. It takes so long for the books to get back on the shelves that anxious library customers are searching the trucks for checked-in books not yet shelved.

The library gets the prepublication list of books to be reviewed in the *New York Times Book Review* and orders them promptly. When the new books arrive, the mailroom staff open the boxes, check the packing slips, and put the books on the shelf to be processed. Customers are disappointed to discover that they cannot check out any of the reviewed books for two more weeks.

What can be done to make these customers happier? Process improvement to the rescue!

The importance of a user-centered approach to library services is becoming widely accepted within libraries and beyond. Whatever that user is called—patron, customer, library user—and whatever the library is called—information center, library media service, learning resources center, research center, information commons—the library must surprise and delight the customer with prompt, friendly, efficient service that meets the need of the moment.

For several years, Sara Laughlin and her associates, Ray Wilson and Denise Shockley, have worked with libraries in several states, offering training in process improvement and showing them how they can improve the work they do to meet the needs and expectations of their customers. It all begins with teams of library staff taking a systems approach to what occurs in the library: identifying customers of the system, identifying and measuring the processes involved in the system, reducing variation in how the work is done, adopting the best-known way, and continuing to measure and improve. It ends with the customers noticing the improvements.

These efforts can and do work for what might be thought of as small systems such as the shelving problem or the slow processing mentioned above, and they can also work on a grand scale for the whole library. As staff change their thinking and develop a systems and processes approach to their work, rapid-cycle improvements show up in many places. The sharp-eyed will recognize the influence of W. Edwards Deming in this approach—his notions of continuously assessing and improving systems work for libraries just as well as they do for manufacturing plants.

From 2004 to 2006, the NY3Rs Association (the nine regional, multitype library networks in New York State), supported in part by Federal Library Services and Technology Act funds awarded to the New York State Library by the Federal Institute of Museum and Library Services, sponsored three series of workshops presented by Laughlin, Shockley, and Wilson called "Continuous Assessment, Continuous Improvement." Each series of workshops was held in three locations across the state; in all, 219 people attended, representing teams from eighty-one libraries. This litany of numbers does not do justice to the effect of this training on the participating libraries. The success stories coming from the participating teams from public, academic, and special libraries indicated a wide range of process improvements. Not only did the work processes improve and impact the customers, but library staff had a renewed sense of energy and pride in their work and their libraries.

This book joins *Process Mastering* (Wilson and Harsin 1998) and *The Library's Continuous Improvement Fieldbook: 29 Ready-to-Use Tools* (Laughlin et al. 2003) in a must-have set of books for those who want to transform their libraries and join others in the business of surprising and delighting customers.

Jean Currie
Executive Director
South Central Regional Library Council
Ithaca, NY

Preface

When we (with coauthor Denise Shockley) began writing *The Library's Continuous Improvement Fieldbook: 29 Ready-to-Use Tools* in 2003, we referred to it as the "first book." It was a way for us to set boundaries and keep from biting off more than we could chew. It was a good place to start, we reasoned. We knew the tools were easy to use and changed the way people worked together. We had some experience using the tools with teams from libraries, and we could tell their stories to help explain and encourage wider use by other libraries. But we knew that using the tools alone would not result in dramatic improvements of quality in libraries. For this, a much more comprehensive, systemic strategy would be needed. We'll write another book later, we convinced ourselves.

Over the intervening three years, we've realized that some of the other pieces necessary to support a system of continuous improvement in a library are already available elsewhere. We did not need to write a book on establishing mission, vision, and values or on communicating with customers. There are plenty of excellent resources for these essential "big picture" pieces.

This, then, is the "second book." It is based on these premises: a library is a system made up of interrelated processes; the processes (and not the people) account for the vast majority of results; and the processes can be continually improved. It further posits that the people who work in the process are the most likely to be able to make improvements. We lay out the strategies and tools necessary to identify, study, and improve library processes. In any type or size of library. With library employees. Within months. Without additional funding or staff.

We know now that this system of process improvement works and that it can have a transformative impact on libraries. We hope that those interested in improving their libraries will find *The Quality Library* easy to understand and will be able to put it to work. It is our dream that we will walk into a transformed library some day and see dog-eared and sticky-noted copies of this volume, process masters and data showing improvements posted near work stations, and teams of library staff studying customer feedback and discussing the next process improvements.

Acknowledgments

Writing a book is never as easy as it looks. This volume began as an effort to document the process improvement methods we have been using with libraries for the past few years. Our clients' inventiveness in finding time to meet and study their own processes has been unfailing. Their discoveries, as they gathered data and talked to each other and to their customers, have been nothing less than revolutionary, as they have questioned, tested, and documented the performance of systems often unchanged in decades. Their successes—in terms of time saved, errors reduced, and customer service improved—have been nothing short of amazing. We have learned from each of the teams. We thank them.

To the teams from libraries who worked with us to tell their stories in this book, we owe a special debt of gratitude:

Benton County (IN) Public Library

Bobst Library, New York University

Crandall Public Library, Glen Falls, NY

Edward G. Miner Library, University of Rochester (NY) Medical College

Evans Library, Fulton-Montgomery Community College, Johnstown, NY

Indiana Library Federation

Kendallville (IN) Public Library

Lawrenceburg (IN) Public Library

Michigan City (IN) Public Library

Mishawaka-Penn-Harris (IN) Public Library

Monroe County (IN) Public Library

Mooresville (IN) Public Library

Pace University Library, New York City and Westchester, NY

Penfield Library, SUNY–Oswego, Oswego, NY

Sojourner Truth Library, SUNY–New Paltz, New Paltz, NY

Van Wagenen Library, SUNY–Cobleskill, Cobleskill, NY

Vigo County (IN) Public Library

Witherill Library, Cazenovia College, Cazenovia, NY

This book would have been much drier reading without the real stories from real libraries. Their directors also deserve thanks, for they provided time away from the desk, offered support when it was needed, and risked trusting their staff to test new ideas for improving their processes.

Thanks especially to Jean Currie, South Central Regional Library Council in Ithaca, New York, whose three LSTA grants allowed us to work with nearly one hundred teams of library staff in New York State; and to Nancy Dowell, Vigo County Public Library in Terre Haute, Indiana; David Eisen, Mishawaka-Penn-Harris Public Library in Mishawaka, Indiana; and Linda Kolb at the Indiana Library Federation, each of whom took a chance by funding our visits and allowing staff teams to participate. Many of the stories come from their libraries.

As always, our families missed us as we spent hours writing and rewriting.

Cindy Wilson and Donna Rinckel are the very best proofreaders on our team, and we thank them. Our editors at ALA have been patient and supportive despite our snail-like pace. All the errors that remain are ours.

Introduction

This book is for library administrators and library employees who want to improve their libraries by improving their processes. Improving processes does not require fancy consultants, advanced degrees, specialized equipment, or additional hours in the day. We have seen dramatic improvements in a very short time in public libraries with five staff members and in academic libraries with scores of staff on several campuses.

We are especially indebted to the paradigm-shifting work of W. Edwards Deming and the people from many disciplines and work contexts who have applied and expanded his concepts over the past fifty years. We find them startlingly new and endlessly thought provoking.

Although plenty of other authors have addressed workflow mapping and other forms of organizational streamlining within libraries, Deming's approach (and ours) is distinctive in its focus on

- understanding the library as a system
- focusing on meeting customer requirements
- locating responsibility and authority for improvement among employee teams
- using statistical techniques to measure results and reduce variation
- continuously improving processes to improve outcomes

BENEFITS OF PROCESS IMPROVEMENT

This book provides a method that allows employees to identify and improve mission-critical processes in the library. It provides tools for employees and managers to gather ongoing, process-level data that empower them to make better decisions and to quantify improved effectiveness for funding and governing bodies.

Library employees will benefit by

- focusing on customer requirements and understanding how their work contributes to pleasing customers
- working with colleagues on improving the processes with which they are most familiar
- gathering data to study and improve their processes
- becoming involved in sharing ideas for improvement in an orderly way
- making their jobs more fulfilling and less frustrating

The library as an organization will benefit by learning from its current processes and continually improving them through

- gaining a clear understanding of who the external and internal customers are for its processes, what they want, and how the processes affect them
- identifying all the processes included in the library and determining which ones are key processes
- identifying who the library's external and internal suppliers are and what the library's processes need from them
- standardizing processes and reducing variation in processes across library employees, locations, and hours
- focusing the library's limited time and resources by identifying key processes for improvement
- identifying unnecessary tasks and processes and eliminating them
- continually improving processes to reduce waiting/turnaround time for customers and costly errors and rework for staff

The library will also benefit from improved employee participation, by

- shortening training time for new employees
- increasing ownership of processes by those who work in them every day
- freeing employees and managers from daily firefighting so they can do more important work
- involving employees at all levels in improving processes without engendering resistance
- discovering hidden talent and passion among staff members

OVERVIEW OF THE BOOK, WITH A FLOWCHART

Figure I-1 is a flowchart that summarizes the major steps in improving library processes. As you continue through the book, you'll be following these general steps.

In chapter 1, we offer a brief overview of the principles that underlie Deming's philosophy of systems thinking and continuous improvement in order to set the context for understanding process improvement. We offer a graphic tool called a "system map" through which employees can picture the library system, including its mission, vision, values, measures, suppliers, inputs, processes, outputs, customers, and feedback loops.

In chapter 2, we define a process as a series of interrelated tasks. We outline a method for engaging employees in identifying processes that are key to achieving the library's goals and assessing the condition of these key processes.

Once a process or processes are chosen, chapter 3 provides a method for standardizing processes called a "process master," which incorporates a series of exercises that help the library team identify all the tasks in a process, consider what customers want from the process and what the process needs from suppliers, identify and document key tasks, and list tools, supplies, equipment, and information required by the process. Remarkably enough, the team often makes substantial improvement to the process during process mastering, even though the emphasis at this point is on simply documenting the process as it is.

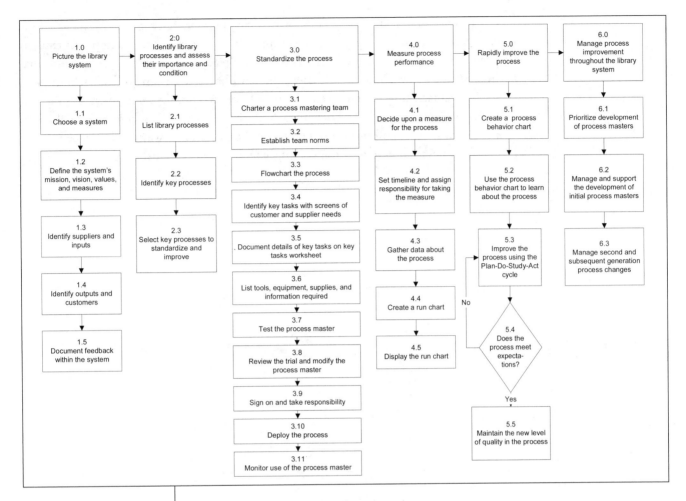

Figure I-1 Flowchart of process improvement.

Chapter 4 addresses the measurement of processes, a paradigm shift from most current library measures. By the end of the chapter, the team has chosen a measure, collected points of data, plotted them on a graph, and found their average.

In chapter 5, team members use three questions to guide their work in rapid improvement of the process. They agree on "What are we trying to do?" and on "How will we know if a change is an improvement?" They ask, "What improvements might we try?" and brainstorm ideas for improving and agree upon a few to try. As they implement the trial, they track results. At the end of a cycle, they display the results in a "process behavior chart" using straightforward statistics to decide if the process has improved enough to meet customer needs and expectations. If not, they begin the rapid improvement cycle again.

Chapter 6 addresses questions of managing process improvement at the organizational level, including data management resources and leadership imperatives.

In each chapter, stories from libraries, gathered during our consulting projects, demonstrate the practical use of these tools and techniques and their impact on reducing mistakes and increasing customer satisfaction. Comprehensive lists of library processes and suggested measures collected during our five years of work with libraries are included as appendixes.

In our combined seventy years of participating and leading improvement efforts within, among, and for organizations, supporting libraries in process improvement has been the most satisfying work of all. We have already witnessed complete transformation within a few libraries. In many others we have seen teams of staff taking pride in the dramatic process improvements they have accomplished and teaching others to improve their processes. We know that these libraries are seeking customer feedback in new, creative ways and incorporating it into their decisions. We have evidence that the communities they serve notice and appreciate the improvements.

| # The Continuous Improvement Approach

Everywhere we turn we hear librarians complaining. Complaining about their staff, their boards, and their customers. Worrying about their budgets. Struggling with technology. Staying late and wondering why they are not recognized for the work they do. Each one of the complaints is enough to send any librarian home with nerves ajangle. Considered together, they are truly overwhelming.

The time has come for a new approach to managing libraries. In this book, we offer a set of tools and strategies for improving library processes that we believe holds the key to understanding the library as a system, aligning the work of staff, saving time and money, and increasing customer satisfaction.

In this chapter, let us set the stage for process improvement by reviewing the challenges to libraries and the opportunities offered by continuous improvement, summarizing the principles of continuous improvement, and picturing the library system by creating a system map.

CHALLENGES TO LIBRARIES

Local decision makers and directors of libraries in the early twenty-first century face three challenges: increased competition for funding, escalating customer expectations, and rapidly changing and complex technology environments. Each of the three also offers opportunities, when they are viewed through the lens of continuous improvement.

Increased Competition for Limited Funding

Pressure is mounting for libraries to demonstrate their value to their funders and constituents. Many libraries still depend on "how much" and "how many" input figures such as collection size and facility square footage or output statistics including circulation, gate count, and program attendance. Recently, some have responded with return-on-investment calculations to show that their library (or the libraries in a whole state) has added value in excess of the budget dollars invested (e.g., Barron et al. 2005; Florida Department of State 2005; Seattle Public Library and Foundation 2005).

When funding is cut, libraries have often responded with incremental cuts to hours, staff, and book budgets or with elimination of entire programs or branches. All too often the libraries have been forced to react quickly, without much warning.

Even in less dire circumstances, where the library's funding is stable or growing modestly, the other two conditions—escalating customer expectations and rapid changes in technology—may complicate allocation of scarce resources.

On the other hand, libraries do receive a substantial amount of funding to carry out important work. Using continuous improvement tools and strategies, they can reconnect with their essential purposes, refocus their work on the services most important to customers, collect a body of evidence that they are producing positive outcomes for them, and sometimes save substantial sums by reducing mistakes that necessitate costly rework.

Escalating Customer Expectations

Customers' expectations are driven by their experiences in the other parts of their lives—where they can purchase a plane ticket or reserve a hotel room online by themselves, go to the grocery or drugstore in the middle of the night, and drink gourmet coffee while reading a magazine. They expect the same levels of service from their libraries:

Customers want current, accurate information. Many customers are becoming savvy information users, but others still need a high level of support to benefit from the vast array of information resources. This wide spread in customer abilities causes a kind of schizophrenia among public service managers, who are trying to support self-service options for some and still offer full service for others. The situation is no different for libraries than for banks or bookstores, where some customers want to handle their own transactions online and others still want friendly service in a neighborhood location.

Customers expect convenient, 24/7 service. They want to check their accounts, renew their books, or place or check the status of an interlibrary loan request whenever they have time. They want to pick up and return materials at locations they frequent and on their own schedules.

Customers want services designed just for them. They would like to receive messages when their favorite author publishes a new book, when a program is offered for their children, and just before their materials are due. They expect services to be delivered in the language they speak by culturally attuned staff.

Customers want reliable service. No matter what time of day or what location they visit (online or in person), they expect to receive the same level of service—the same courtesy, the same offerings, the same timeliness.

Customers expect high-quality service in comfortable surroundings. They want to be treated well as they drink coffee, sit in comfortable chairs, meet friends, listen to music, have quiet space, and make phone calls.

Viewed through the continuous improvement lens, these escalating customer expectations offer many opportunities for libraries. They focus new attention on the necessity of gathering regular feedback from customers and potential customers. For too long, libraries have concentrated on their own outgoing messages (bookmarks, posters, press releases, newsletters, annual reports) and relied on informal conversations with regular users at the desk for feedback. They have no intentional way to collect customer feedback, study it, and take action. They can produce no evidence about overall customer satisfaction with service or about the outcomes the library has produced. Once the library has a regular stream of feedback coming from customers, it is able to identify which services and processes need improvement. As it begins to listen more intentionally and to make the improvements customers have requested, the library can identify further improvements that will be attractive to its customers and can increase levels of satisfaction by implementing the improvements.

Rapidly Changing and Complex Technological Environments

Many of the funding challenges and rising customer expectations are exacerbated by technology. Technology requires funding. Even though technology is acknowledged to be mission critical in any library, support for hardware and software upgrades and staff training is too often still dependent on grants and other external, one-time funding. When technology funds are integrated into the library's operating budget, they compete with salary, materials, and facilities needs. Customers, though, expect the library to utilize current technology. As the director of one small library recently quipped, "We don't have a problem knowing what our customers want. They ask us for it every day."

Technology available to others provides powerful, well-funded competition for the library. When students who are writing papers can stay home and find current information online, what motivation do they have for visiting the library? How else can they become aware of the expertise and the other resources the library offers? When library governing boards themselves question whether the library is necessary, what response can the library make? Libraries, which have long enjoyed an apparent monopoly on basic information sources and services, must now face this competition and differentiate their services.

Within the continuous improvement framework, technology offers potential solutions to the funding and customer challenges. It allows the library to gather, analyze, and put to immediate use a steady stream of data. Data on customer preferences and library performance can help the library identify services to be offered and key processes to be improved. Process improvement results in reduced response time, fewer errors, and strengthened interconnections among the individual processes in the library, which frequently results in direct cost savings. Technology can help the library understand its individual customers and customize experiences for them, far beyond what could be supported in the earlier manual environment. It helps staff improve communications inside the library and out.

PRINCIPLES OF CONTINUOUS IMPROVEMENT

The continuous improvement framework we describe in this book is based on the principles of internationally renowned consultant W. Edwards Deming. Deming's principles have been successfully applied in business, industry, government, and education, and to a limited extent in libraries. Applying them requires thinking about libraries in an entirely new way—as a *system* with suppliers, processes, and customers, and with data and feedback informing every part of the system. It requires understanding the purpose of the system and working to improve the system.

After World War II, Deming led Japanese industry in applying new principles of management and helped them revolutionize their quality and productivity. Over the next forty-three years, Deming wrote and lectured about his principles; he conducted hundreds of seminars in which he challenged thousands of participants from business and industry to discard the traditional methods of management and adopt his methods, and he involved them in exercises that served as simple but unforgettable demonstrations of his principles. By the time of his death in 1993 at the age of ninety-three, Deming was also credited with transforming American manufacturing so that it could challenge the very Japanese quality standards he had elevated so many years before. In his *Out of the Crisis,* he described this transformation as a paradigm shift: "Transformation of American style of management is not a job of reconstruction, nor is it revision. It requires a whole new structure, from foundation upward" (Deming 1986, ix).

Deming believed that his principles offered great promise for not-for-profit organizations as well as for business and industry. His principles continue to have wide impact; in the past two decades or so, they have been increasingly incorporated in government, education, and social service contexts.[1] But the library world has been slower to embrace these principles (O'Neil 1994). After a flurry of interest in the early 1990s, interest waned, perhaps because traditional structures were deeply embedded and the impetus to change had not reached a crisis point. In the current climate of increased accountability, funding crunches, technological complexity, and customer demands that most libraries face, Deming's approach is attracting new interest, as libraries search for solutions. A brief overview of his principles sets the stage for understanding process improvement.

VISUALIZING A SYSTEM: RAY'S MOBILE

Several years ago I (not an artist to be sure) decided to participate in an Artist's Way group (Cameron 1992). As an outgrowth of our time together, the group challenged each of us to do an art project. Having always been interested in Calder mobiles, I chose to design and build a mobile. It was a simple but fascinating project. As you might imagine, there is care required to cut and bend metal wires and add fins and seek to get the balance and look you want. As the mobile takes shape, you realize that every additional arm you add to the mobile is dependent on the ones that have gone before. When you are finished and the mobile is hanging by a thread, all the arms and fins are free to move when disturbed by breezes or fingers.

Some months later as I was pondering how I could help people visualize a system, I hit on the idea of using the mobile to represent a system. Everything is connected to everything. Whenever anything moves, the relationships between all the parts of the mobile change.

If you can think of your library as a super-complicated mobile with thousands of arms and fins and hundreds if not thousands of disturbances affecting it every day, you can begin to get a sense of how everything that happens in a library affects everything else—maybe in a small or large way, maybe now or many years later.

The Library Is a System

When Deming looked at the traditional organization chart, he realized that it was a picture of a system designed to please the director (figure 1-1). Customers of the organization are implicit, not even included in the chart. In order for a person at the bottom of the chart—usually the frontline worker with direct customer contact—to communicate with another frontline worker, he/she has to send a message up the chain of command, over to the next line, and back down. The message gets distorted along the way (as in the telephone game). It takes a long time. It doesn't empower the worker. Managers must know everything. The organization succeeds only if there are no exceptions and every individual does his/her job as directed to satisfy the person above. Quality is the result of individual (or team) effort.

Look familiar? Most libraries probably have organizational charts that look much like this one. Is it any wonder that customers are sometimes an afterthought?

Deming described the organization as a system and drew a different picture, similar to figure 1-2. In this view, customers are shown at the right-hand end of the system, receiving products and services from the system. Suppliers and the inputs they contribute to the system are shown on the left. In the center are the processes that produce the organization's products and ser-

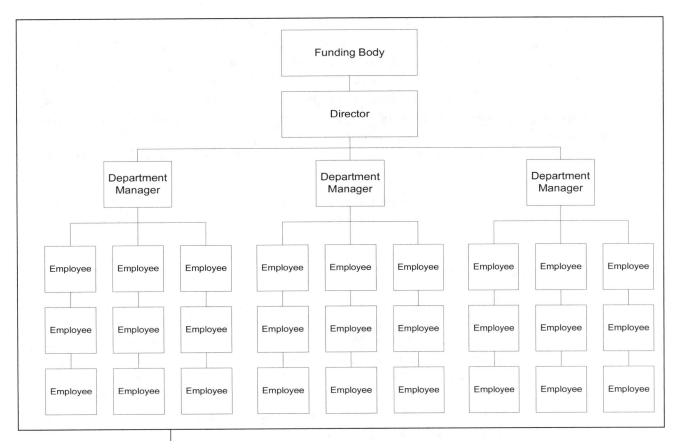

Figure 1-1 Traditional organizational view of a library. The director and department managers oversee the work of the employees; customers are not visible on the chart.

vices. The processes included in the center line are those that lead directly to products and services for customers. In a library, those processes might include selecting and ordering items, cataloging items, circulating items, answering questions, presenting programs, and teaching classes. Supporting processes include all the other things the library does, which might not be visible to customers or important to providing direct service. These processes might not even be missed if they weren't carried out for a few days (although eventually they would be). Some examples of supporting processes: cleaning the library, updating software, hiring and training staff, preparing the budget, and paying the bills.

Feedback loops connect the elements; on the right of our system picture, customers and customer research provide feedback for the design and redesign of the system; on the left, the system provides feedback to its suppliers in order to improve the quality of inputs. Deming said, "Improvement of quality envelops the entire production line, from incoming materials to the consumer, and redesign of product and service for the future" (1986, 4).

Libraries are not factories, it is true, but many of the processes that libraries employ day-in and day-out are production oriented. Think, for example, about ordering and preparing items for circulation. Isn't that similar to ordering for any operation? Doesn't design and redesign of your services—from your website to your integrated library system to your programming—influence the quality your customers receive? Of course it does, so don't let the business terminology keep you from thinking about the library as a system.

Figure 1-2 illustrates some key system principles:

The system is focused on pleasing customers rather than on pleasing supervisors. All the elements in the system contribute to the desired outcome of pleasing customers. Improving the processes by which the system delivers products and services and improving the quality of supplies entering the system can help with that. Getting feedback from customers is an important way to learn whether the system is meeting their current expectations and what opportunities they see for improvement.

Deming pointed out that systems must produce products and services customers want:

> It is a mistake to suppose that efficient production of product and service can with certainty keep an organization solvent and ahead of competition. It is possible and in fact fairly easy for an organization to go downhill and out of business making the wrong product or offering the wrong type of service, even though everyone in the organization performs with devotion, employing statistical methods and every other aid that can boost efficiency. (1986, 26)

Recently, business experts have stressed that customers are an important source of innovation (e.g., Christensen et al. 2004; McGregor 2006; Nussbaum 2005).

System performance depends on the interaction among parts of the system. "The performance of a system is not the sum of the performance of its parts taken separately, but the product of their interaction" (Ackoff 1994, 23). Each part of the system affects every other part, even though the effect is not always immediately evident. Systems can be complex and problems tend to have multiple causes. Technical processes affect people processes, and vice versa.

Think, for example, of the quality of bindings on books when the library receives them or of the indexing in a full-text database. Both affect the quality the library can deliver to its customers. How does the library typically deal with poor-quality bindings? Sometimes it changes vendors, but more frequently it wastes valuable library resources. If the binding is obviously bad when the book comes out of the shipping box, the library

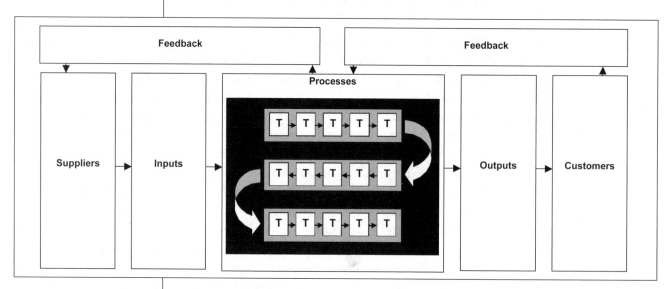

Figure 1-2 The library as a system. Suppliers provide inputs to the library. Inside the library, the inputs are transformed through various interrelated processes into outputs for customers. Customers and suppliers give feedback to the library system, which it uses to improve its own processes and those of its suppliers.

might return it to the vendor or attempt to repair it—before it has even circulated once. If the damage is not evident, the book might go through the library's preparation processes and be checked out by a customer before the damage is discovered. If it comes back to the library missing an entire signature and the library notices that, it has to be withdrawn and perhaps replaced. If the library doesn't notice, and the book is checked out by another customer, the customer is annoyed to find part of the text missing and his/her assessment of the library's quality suffers. It's the 1-10-100 rule in action. It might cost $1 more for the vendor to produce a better binding. It costs $10 (think about the postage, the staff time, and the delay for the customer) for the library to discover the faulty work and return the item. It costs $100 (including the postage, staff time, reorder costs, and loss of reputation) when the customer has checked out the book and can't use it.

Similarly, the quality of indexing defines and limits access to the articles contained in a full-text database. Once the library has subscribed to the database, it is dependent on the index to help customers find content. If the indexer misses indexing a key concept, it would take only a minute to add it. Once the index is produced without the missing concept, it is virtually impossible for a searcher to find that article by searching for the concept.

The system—and not the people in the system—is responsible for the overwhelming majority of system results. By the end of his life, Deming allocated 96 percent of system results to common causes (i.e., those that are routine variations within the system) and 4 percent to special causes (those caused by unusual, exceptional circumstances) (Joiner 1994, 34). For more on common causes and special causes of variation, see chapter 5.

For most librarians we know, this is a startling concept. But all you have to do is follow the progress of almost any service in the library to realize how many individuals, departments, and processes are involved. Think about a library staff member helping a customer find a particular title. The staff member is totally dependent on the processes in place in the library, including the acquisitions, cataloging, technical services, circulation, and shelving processes. As an individual, the staff member often joins the library with substantial background knowledge and skills, but without reliable processes in place answering this simple request would be next to impossible. Finding a particular title in the library depends on the selections process identifying it, the acquisitions process ordering it promptly and accurately, the cataloging process (in the technical services department, at the vendor, or elsewhere) describing it and providing multiple points of access, the technical services process accurately labeling the item, and the shelving process putting it in the right place. In the electronic world, the librarian is dependent on similar processes, but interactions among processes are more difficult to see and frequently occur at least partially outside the library. If any of these processes—physical or electronic—is weak or fails, it weakens the ability of any staff member to help the customer. Blaming an individual responsible for any task in the process won't help improve the system. Indeed, improving a single process won't help. To improve the system, you must improve the processes and the interactions among the processes.

Every System Has an Aim

Deming stated that a system must have an aim that is clear to everyone in the system and includes the purpose or mission of the system and its plans for the future (2000, 51). For libraries, the aim is expressed in a Constancy of Purpose statement that includes four elements: mission, vision, values, and measures.[2]

Mission

The mission of the library describes who the library serves, what they receive from the library, and for what purpose. It is the promise the library makes to its customers and funders. Here are two examples:

> The Monroe County (IN) Public Library offers equitable access to information, a place to gather, and opportunities for lifelong learning, enrichment, and enjoyment.

> The Edward G. Miner Library provides the University of Rochester Medical Center (URMC) and the greater Rochester community with resources, expertise and an inviting space to support health, discovery, teaching and learning.

Vision

The vision describes the library in its future perfect state, assuming that the mission is being carried out in the most perfect way. It is a word picture that helps the library and others in the community imagine what is possible. The vision of the Edward G. Miner Library at the University of Rochester Medical Center (see mission statement above) is a good example:

> We have a clean, secure, friendly, comfortable facility that embraces both latest technologies and natural elements. Skylights and outdoor seating enhance the bright, open, spacious, and user-friendly layout. The prevailing feeling is contemporary and energetic, and the welcoming aroma of coffee permeates the air. Our customers can choose their preferred study environment—interactive areas that encourage collaboration, communication, and group learning; or quiet study spaces that are serene, warm, and comfortable.
>
> Health Science Libraries & Technologies staff enjoy their work, take pride in their professionalism and expertise, and lead the way in introducing cutting-edge computer technologies to the URMC. Staff workspace is uncluttered, spacious, and flexible, comfortably accommodating individual or interactive group work. We greet customers warmly and treat them with courtesy and respect, whether their presence is "real" or "virtual."
>
> We provide the information our users need—whenever and wherever they need it—to teach, learn, conduct research, and provide patient care. Extensive online resources are easy to locate on our reliable, accurate, and intuitive web site, and linking software allows customers to easily move from resource to resource. The libraries and HSLT-supported classrooms and computer labs are completely wireless.
>
> Patients, their families, and members of the public find comprehensive consumer health information and friendly, knowledgeable staff in our latest branch library—the Strong Health Knowledge Center located in the hospital's lobby. As part of the health care team, we provide digital consumer health information via bedside computers to patients who have been admitted to the hospital, to help them with their health care decision-making.

Values

Values clarify the enduring principles for which the library stands. Values are applied by the library as it makes decisions. The values have most power when they guide how everyone in the organization—board, staff, volunteers—makes decisions and treats each other and customers. The values of the Edward G. Miner Library were developed by their staff:

Initiative and Innovation. We support creativity, reasonable risk taking, the application of innovative technologies, and leadership at all levels.

Personal Integrity and Respect. We display mutual respect, caring, and truthfulness toward each other, our customers, and our collaborators.

Customer Service. Meeting customer needs is our highest priority, and we interact with customers in a friendly, caring, and courteous manner.

Partnerships. We work together for the best possible outcome—with each other, with customers, and with other collaborators within and outside the University of Rochester Medical Center.

Life-Long Learning. We create and sustain an environment conducive to continuous individual and organizational learning.

Responsibility. We each assume personal responsibility for the success of the group and our mission.

Optimism. We aspire to provide a joyful environment, where we work with enthusiasm and a positive attitude.

Privacy. We protect the privacy of customers and co-workers to the fullest extent of the law.

Intellectual Freedom. We promote and protect every individual's right to find information, read, study and learn.

Measures

High-level measurements allow the library's decision makers and stakeholders to follow the library's progress. Two current frameworks for high-level measures are outcome-based evaluation, based on the United Way's groundbreaking work on measuring the impact of social services, and Balanced Scorecard, used by an increasing number of government units.[3] Measures of processes are included in both frameworks. Even though it is difficult work, it is important to begin to discuss and choose measures. In chapter 4 we describe how to measure the current performance of library processes; in chapter 5 we describe how to use the measures to track process improvement.

In this book, we don't linger over creating Constancy of Purpose statements, since many excellent sources exist, but it is critically important to remember that every system needs an aim and that the aim, clearly expressed in a Constancy of Purpose statement, is a powerful tool for unifying staff and focusing resources (see, e.g., Wallace 2004).

The System Can Continually Be Improved

To improve the system, wrote Deming, improve the processes in the system, beginning with the design stage and continuing through the system. As products or services move through one process after another, continual reduction of waste and improvement of quality in every process will improve results.

Deming suggested several actions to improve the system, including reducing variation, improving upstream processes, minimizing inspections, and investing in people.

Reducing Variation

"Life is variation," wrote Deming. Educated as an engineer and mathematician, Deming had struggled to understand and control variation for years. He began to employ

Jenny Draper, director of the Kendallville Public Library, related the following story:

My library is part of a library consortium made up of eighteen libraries in a six-county area of northeastern Indiana. This six-county area is also the geographic funding area of a local foundation. The consortium has worked closely with this foundation to fund staff training and children's art programs for all the libraries involved.

Recently the foundation approached the consortium with a proposal they wanted the group to pursue. A committee was formed to actually put the proposal together, and I was part of that committee. The committee met several times and discussed ideas and scope for several hours each time. We all took pages of notes, filled pages on the flipchart and of course talked and talked. But for some reason, we could not get the actual grant proposal written.

Subsequently, I attended a marketing workshop and was called upon to state my library's mission, which I did—because it is short, and I can remember it exactly. Several times throughout the presentation I was asked to repeat our mission. The third time I stated the mission out loud, the light bulb came on. The reason I couldn't put the grant proposal together was that the committee was proposing activities outside my library's mission.

At this point I couldn't wait to get back to the library and attack the proposal again. I pulled out all of my notes, fired up the computer, and got started. Keeping in mind what our library's mission was, I wrote the proposal in two hours. With the background work already done and the mission in front of me, it was a breeze. And it all made sense. The proposal was submitted and approved, and the consortium is now implementing the program. What a difference the mission statement made.

statistical techniques to study variation in order to understand how well processes were performing and to predict the future. He knew that variation could not be eliminated, but still he believed that processes could be improved if variation could be understood. If processes were stable, managers would know when variation was within a predictable range and when it was not, and they would intervene only when variation was outside that predictable range.

Deming learned that reducing variation would always improve the results of the system. Think about variation in the number of people eating in restaurants between the weekend and weekdays and you'll begin to see that those Tuesday family specials are efforts to reduce variation. For the restaurant manager, variation means difficulties in predicting how much food to order from suppliers and how many employees to schedule, resulting in food waste, complaints from customers about long waits, and lost profits. For customers, variation means long lines and poor service on busy nights and reduced menu choices on less busy nights. Reducing the day-to-day variation in the number of customers makes the restaurant run more smoothly.

It is easy to think of examples of variation in the library: the number of customers per day, the temperature in various parts of the building, the number of books checked out or returned every day, or the number of hits to the website. It is also easy to assume that every one of these instances occurs in isolation, motivated by the whims of customers.

We don't control the number of hits to the website, you might say. It varies. Of course, that's true, but if you were to plot on a chart the number of hits per hour over a period of weeks or months, certain predictable patterns would emerge. When the website was brand new, there would be wild differences from one day to another, but after a while you would begin to notice more hits in the middle of the day and fewer in the middle of the night, more hits during the week and fewer on the weekend, and fewer hits during holiday periods. Before long, the points on the chart would form a pattern. Without applying any fancy calculations, you could discern an average, with the other points clustered above and below it. You could identify any dramatically lower points and probably attribute those to a day when the system was down or there was a major holiday. You could see obviously higher points and perhaps remember that they occurred on a day when you sent an e-mail announcing a popular new service or offered several library orientation sessions in the computer lab.

The chart of website hits is a perfect picture of variation in your system. If the system is stable, the patterns will fluctuate in a predictable pattern. As you look at the chart, you will notice two things: the average number of hits and the amount of variation. You might or might not be happy with the average. If you're not, you might decide to take some actions to increase the number—perhaps doing some promotion of the site or adding more content. You might or might not be happy with the variation. If you're not, you might also take action to decrease the variation—perhaps planning regular promotions and content upgrades to align with periods when traffic is lighter.

Variation also occurs in the people processes in the library. Consider the variation when shelvers have different understandings of accuracy. Or when customers who call at different times or into different locations get different answers to the same question. Or when it takes one circulation desk staffer four times longer than another to explain library services to a new patron. Or when the gift book selectors are swamped with donations one week and have none the next. Consider how variation is evident even in meetings—from one committee to another, or from one meeting to another. Each of these situations may put a strain on the processes of the library and offers opportunities for improvement.

But, you say, we are creative people, and we don't want to march in lockstep. Won't reducing variation make our jobs boring and routine? Quite the contrary. The very work of reducing variation creates opportunities for creativity. As teams meet to master their process, they realize that not everyone does the process tasks the same way. They often discover tasks that are repeated or are unnecessary. They identify shortcuts and new software in use in one area that they can adopt in other areas. They see immediate results, just from reducing the obvious variation in process tasks. In fact, the problem that many organizations face as they adopt continuous improvement is managing the tremendous creativity that it unleashes—a problem that many library leaders would be happy to have.

Improving Upstream Processes

It is obvious from the figure 1-2 system drawing that the quality of inputs is a determining factor at every step. Deming suggested building long-term relationships with fewer suppliers, in order to improve the quality of inputs to the system, rather than awarding business on price tag alone. An ongoing relationship is preferable, according to Deming, because building relationships with suppliers is an expensive and disruptive operation that introduces variation and adds cost.

Think about the total cost of changing from one external supplier to another, whether it is the library's book jobber, database vendor, cleaning contractor, payroll processor, or insurance underwriter. First, the library must select a new supplier, usually through a formal bid process, which takes substantial library staff time and vendor staff time. Second, the library must orient the new supplier to the library's specific requirements, expectations, facilities and technical systems, and personnel, another time-consuming enterprise. Finally, there is the learning period during which both library and supplier answer questions and resolve issues until the system is running smoothly.

What can a library do to improve input from external suppliers? One approach is to work with an existing supplier to improve its products or services. In this scenario, the supplier is already familiar with the library's procedures, and its staff has developed relationships with library staff. The library might gather data about problems it is experiencing with the supplies it receives from the supplier. The library might also encourage other libraries to do the same and set up a procedure to ensure that they are all collecting data in the same way. When the library or a group of libraries presents the vendor with data documenting the problem, the vendor is much more likely to take action to fix the problem. At the same time, the vendor's knowledge of the library's specific requirements has increased, and it can use that knowledge to improve its own processes. The quality of inputs is improved without the expense of switching suppliers.

What about situations in which the library cannot influence external suppliers? Consider a seemingly minor process in a public library—selecting gift books. The suppliers of the gift books are individuals. Sometimes they bring the books into the library, singly or by the bagful. Sometimes people drop them into the book drop, where they are mingled with the library books being returned. Sometimes the library receives boxes and truckloads of books when someone cleans out an attic. How can the library have any impact on these suppliers? After all, they don't work for the library. They don't communicate with each other. Their actions are unpredictable.

The staff of the Vigo County Public Library decided to study this process. They gathered data for a month, during which time the library received more than three thousand usable gift books (note that they didn't count those they discarded), added one-third of them to the collection, and forwarded the remaining two-thirds to the Friends of the Library for sale in their bookstore. When the team calculated the value of the books that would be added over a year, the total nearly equaled the amount the library was spending on paperbacks. Of course, the cost of preparing the books for circulation was high, since they had to be sorted and did not come preprocessed. How could the library improve the process of donation? They considered ways to inform potential donors of the types of books they particularly needed—recent bestsellers, paperback romances, children's books—and those they did not want—back issues of *National Geographic,* moldy books, old textbooks. They planned to initiate a public awareness campaign and keep measures to see if the overall number and percentage of usable books increased.

Inside the library, one process is the internal supplier of another. Here too, upstream processes affect downstream results. It is not uncommon for staff members in one area to spend at least part of every day repairing problems that were created in another area. In one library, the director told us, "We have a full-time person whose job is to fix mistakes." Think, for example, of the time spent in the payroll department trying to decode time-cards that are incomplete or hard to read. Think of the problems caused for the reference staff when books are misshelved. Think of the time wasted when the library's e-mail is down. The methods for improving the quality of supplies received from internal suppliers are the same as those for external suppliers: share clear expectations for quality and provide data on problems.

Minimizing Inspections

Deming urged organizations to cease dependence on inspection to achieve quality, because inspections don't add value but do add cost. Inspections often contribute to variation because inspectors can make mistakes, operational definitions of how to do the inspection are not always clear, and fear of the consequences of inspections colors inspectors' perceptions and decisions.

If inspection must be done, argued Deming, it should be done to gather data for process improvement. And it is even better to improve the processes to the point that they cannot be done incorrectly and therefore obviate the need for inspection.

We have discovered that inspection is widespread in libraries. We visited a library that had participated in our training and saw an example of inspection—and an opportunity to work upstream with internal suppliers. As we were talking to the circulation manager in her office, we noticed that an entire range of shelving behind her desk was full of new books. We asked what they were doing there, because we knew the library had been working on reducing the time spent from receipt to shelving of new books. "I take a look at each one," said the circulation manager. "Isn't that inspection?" we replied. "Well yes, I guess it is. We kept data for a month and decided there were so many errors we should continue inspecting." As we talked, she realized that a team was just beginning work on improving the process that produced the books for the shelf. She gave them the data she had collected as input for their upstream process improvement. The next time we stopped in, she reported that the team had realized that, not only was the department head inspecting, but the circulation worker who did the initial check-in of the item in the main library or branch was also checking the same details. Since the check-in had to be done, they decided to eliminate the department head's inspection.

Investing in the People in the System

Even though the system is responsible for the overwhelming majority of the results, the people in the system still hold the keys to improving it, not through their individual labor but through their knowledge, skills, and understanding of the system. They are the process experts. To improve the system, people must work together in relationships that manage the processes and bridge all the interactions in the system.

Continuous improvement requires active participation as a member of a team (or several teams), regular use of data from processes and customers to make decisions, and attention to process improvement possibilities. These skill sets have not necessarily been included in the education and training received by most library employees. If everybody in the library is to be put to work accomplishing the transformation, then everybody will need to learn the basic tools of continuous improvement. It's not rocket science, but it must be learned.

It may not be the norm of library leaders to feel comfortable empowering employees to take ownership of processes and to allow them to be creative and take risks. For some this will be a bold and difficult step. Likewise, for some employees there may be some hesitation, because they may feel their job or salary is in jeopardy. Therefore, it is critical at the outset for leaders to state clearly that no employees will lose their jobs as a contribution to quality or productivity improvement. Jobs may, however, change.

It is easy to see that, if this practice is carried out, the power of the organization to improve will be multiplied many times. Every activity, every job, and therefore every person will be part of the system and will take part in improving it. In *Beyond Reengineering: How the Process-Centered Organization Is Changing Our Work and Our Lives*, Michael Hammer pointed out how powerful such a simple alignment can be: "Even the most mundane work can be given meaning and value for those who perform it if they understand how it benefits, even in the simplest of ways, the lives of others" (1996, 268).

In chapter 3, we offer a strategy for chartering teams that helps the organization engage the people who do the work in improving their own processes for the benefit of customers. It sounds so simple, but it is amazing how rarely employees have a chance to make suggestions and the authority to try them out.

The best moments usually occur when a person's body or mind is stretched to its limits in voluntary effort to accomplish something difficult and worthwhile. . . . in the long run optimal experiences add up to a sense of mastery—or perhaps better, a sense of participation in determining the content of life—that comes as close to what is usually meant by happiness as anything else we can conceivably imagine.
—Mihaly Csikszentmihalyi (1990, 3-4)

When a library is viewed as a system, it is easy to see that the outputs from one department are the inputs for another; likewise, the customers of one department are the suppliers of another, until the product or service finally reaches the ultimate customer, at which point its quality is the end result of all the departments (and processes, as we shall see) it has passed through.

We believe that, if you try some of the process mastering and improvement exercises suggested in the following chapters, your own experience will support Deming's research. By the time you finish this book, we hope that you'll understand that a library is a system with a purpose, that processes can be improved through the understanding of variation and careful study and implementation of changes, and that employees can and must be empowered to act to improve the system.

PICTURE THE LIBRARY SYSTEM

Although most librarians have an intuitive understanding of the parts of the library system, many find making a picture of the system a thought-provoking (and not necessarily easy) exercise. The system map is the tool we adopted for this purpose.[4] Let's work through the components of the system map in figure 1-3, beginning with the top.

Organization: _____	Team: _____
System Name: _____	Revision Date: _____
Mission:	Values:
Vision:	Measures:

Feedback:		Feedback:

Suppliers:	Inputs:	Processes Primary Processes Supporting Processes	Outputs:	Customers:

Figure 1-3 System map template.

Step 1.1
Choose a system: organization, system name, team, and date.

Drawing the boundary of the system is the first step. Begin with the name of your library and the name of the system you will be describing. For most teams, the initial system map represents the entire library. Some may choose to create a system map for a subsystem within the library, perhaps for a single function or a department. Deciding what to include and where to draw the line may take more deliberation than you expected, since this is a new way of looking at the library and its work. Whatever system or subsystem you choose, add the information to your system map along with the date and names of team members participating in the exercise.

Step 1.2
Define the system's mission, vision, values, and measures.

Earlier in this chapter, we discussed the mission, vision, values, and high-level measures for the system, so you can fill in that section of the system map right away.

Let's now focus on the bottom half of the system map, beginning on the left with suppliers and inputs.

Step 1.3
Identify suppliers and inputs.

Inputs are the raw materials from which the library creates its products and services. Suppliers are the sources of those supplies or inputs. Perhaps the most tangible example of an input is books. The library receives books from a variety of vendors, who are the suppliers. Some may be individual vendors and others may be jobbers. You can probably make a list fairly easily of the types of books and other library materials you physically order and receive (inputs) and the vendors from whom they are purchased (suppliers).

To begin your lists of suppliers and inputs, think about the checks the library writes every month (or at least once a year). What is the library purchasing? From whom?

Some inputs, like information and expertise, are not tangible and don't arrive in a box. Some inputs, like volunteer time or reciprocal agreements, don't show up in the monthly check register. Remember to include these inputs and their suppliers on your list. For example, the volunteers who staff your literacy program supply tutoring expertise and time, but you never write them a check. You may be borrowing items on interlibrary loan (inputs) from neighboring libraries; they are therefore also your suppliers. Your funding body is another supplier, as are the authorities who appoint board members or advisory committee members.

If your list of suppliers or inputs becomes overwhelming, consider listing just categories of suppliers, such as utilities, volunteers, maintenance contractors, and book suppliers, or categories of inputs, for example, office supplies, maintenance supplies, or databases. Or you may want to list only those you consider most important. In figure 1-4, a system map for the Pace University Library, you'll notice that the suppliers are aligned with each input. (Notice that this early version of the system map lacks measures.)

Organization: Pace University Library
Name of System: Pace Library

Team: Assessment Team
Revision Date: April 2004

MISSION

The Pace Library will maintain a physical and virtual environment that promotes learning, supports teaching and scholarship, and fosters lifelong intellectual growth and discovery by providing all members of the Pace community with access to needed library and information resources, research assistance, instruction and guidance in developing the research skills necessary for locating and evaluating information.

VISION

The Library is truly at the center of the campus crossroads. It is an energetic information hub where integrated service delivery offers users one-stop shopping. It is a gateway to globally linked knowledge and information sources as well as the focal point of technology-based learning. Other libraries view us as a model of the information commons in glorious practice and study our operations in the hope of mirroring our success. The library is a learning commons and also a learning incubator facilitating information literacy, media proficiency, technological fluency and innovative teaching and learning modes.

VALUES

Quality Service: A long-term approach to success through customer satisfaction reached by fulfilling the real expectations of library users.

User-Centeredness: Making user expectations a priority and engaging users in assessment to improve library services and resources.

Resourcefulness: Using the varied expertise and talents of a diverse staff to strategically maximize the provision of products and services our users desire.

Teamwork: The willingness to work hard and work cohesively in order to "do what it takes" to keep operations running smoothly.

Integrity: Having solid principles, including reliability and accountability to others, in the performance of our jobs.

MEASURES (to be determined)

Feedback Loops: Telephone; email; mail; formal designated contacts/reps; on-site; consortia negotiations; participation in focus groups; conference vendor exhibits; surveys from university offices & services; committee participation.

Feedback Loops: LibQUAL+; suggestion boxes; pre-instruction & post-instruction assessment; outcomes assessment; conversations with users; email: follow-ups; feedback; unsolicited comments; Web page suggestions form; focus groups; Faculty Liaison committee; occasional surveys of specific populations; Academic Resources committee; accreditation review.

Suppliers

Vendors (YBP)
Vendors, publishers, bookstores
Donors
Vendors (Ebsco)
Vendors, DOIT
Vendors
Other libraries, Pace community
OCLC
Vendors
Vendors
University
University
Government
University
WALDO, Metro, OCLC
Faculty, academic programs
Faculty, students, staff
Faculty, Library, Doc. Delivery
Library users
Faculty, staff, students, WALDO

Inputs

Cataloged books
Uncataloged books
Gift books
Journals
Hardware and software
Multimedia
ILL requests
Cataloging data
Databases
Supplies
Utilities
University regulations
Government regulations
Money
Membership in consortia
Request for instruction session
Recommendations for resources
Materials for reserve
Request for assistance
Request for documentation

Processes

Primary:
Acquire resources (including selection)
Provide research assistance
Catalog resources
Process resources
Shelve materials
Maintain collections—weed, bind, mend, replace lost/missing items
Put materials on reserve: books; E-Res
Assure access to electronic resources: in-house and remotely
Maintain technical infrastructure
Provide technical assistance
Circulate resources
Provide instruction
Share resources—intra campus and interlibrary—as lender and borrower
Create and maintain Web pages—general and class/topic specific

Supporting: (Technical T & Social S)
Train staff T, S
Do preventive maintenance T
Clean the building T
Resolve conflicts S
Evaluate and compensate staff S
Hire staff S
Participate on committees S
Investigate emergent technologies T
Plan and set goals & objectives T, S

Outputs

Books on shelf
E-Books
Databases
Journals in library
Online full-text journals
Reserves—on-shelf and E-Res
Archival materials
Microforms and reader/printers
Multimedia & viewing equipment
Formal instruction sessions
Answers to reference requests—in-person; email; online real time
Blackboard research forums
Books and materials from other libraries & doc. delivery services
Access to technology—in-house and remote access
Working computers
Technical assistance
Web pages—general, class/topic
Online interactive tutorials
Environment/building educational and social events
Faculty development offerings

Customers

Students
Undergrad
Grad
Distance education
Nontraditional—returning/ adult ed.
Students with disabilities
English as a Second Language
Faculty
Full-time
Adjunct
Emeritus
Teaching fellows
Staff
Administration
Alumni PARC
World Trade Institute (WTI)
WALDO faculty
Public
Other libraries
Government and other agencies

Figure 1-4 Organization-wide system map of the Pace University Library.

If you have chosen to make a system map of a function or department within the larger library, you almost certainly have internal suppliers as well as external suppliers. For example, the suppliers for the reference function are the selectors, the acquisitions staff, and shelvers, as well as the training department and payroll department, of course. In figures 1-5 and 1-6, created during staff brainstorming sessions, two libraries used system maps to help them understand subsystems within their overall library system. Figure 1-5, from Crandall Public Library, is a map of the facility system for the library.

In figure 1-6, the system map of the circulation system within the Van Wagenen Library at the State University of New York (SUNY)–Cobleskill, notice the internal suppliers—MultiLIS and the interlibrary loan department—as well as external suppliers including the registrar. The SUNY–Plattsburgh Library is also listed and could be considered internal or external.

Step 1.4
Identify outputs and customers.

This part should be easy. Just get out your latest brochure and make a list of your products and services, right? Maybe. Filling in this part of the system map causes you to think about what it is that customers really want and get from the library. For example, is it just "books"? If so, why don't they go directly to the supplier? Perhaps, after some discussion, you will decide that customers want "free, high-quality books" or "free best sellers." You may find that your final list of outputs is broader and more detailed than your initial notes. Again, don't forget about the intangible outputs, like answers to questions.

If you are struggling with describing your system's outputs, take a look at the three system map examples. The outputs listed by the Pace University Library in figure 1-4 are tangible. Notice that it doesn't list "books" but rather "books on shelf," in recognition of the value the library has added by cataloging and organizing them for easy retrieval. Notice, too, that it frames the outputs in customer language—"answers to reference requests" instead of "reference." In figure 1-5, the Crandall Public Library used a similar approach as it described the outputs of the facility system, such as "clean, ice-free sidewalks." In figure 1-6, the SUNY–Cobleskill Library included an intangible output, "friendliness," on its list.

We use the term "customer" in this volume to mean those individuals or groups who receive a product or service provided by the organization.[5] We frequently find that library staff teams start off with a very global statement, involving something like "everybody" or "taxpayers," and then discover smaller, overlapping groups of customers. Understanding each group and how it relates to the library is an ongoing and important challenge. Here are some customer groups to start your discussion:

- Customers by age group, for example, infants and their parents, toddlers, preschool children, early readers, high school students, retired seniors.
- Customers who use different library products and services, for example, genealogists, investors, light fiction readers, stamp collectors. Referring to your list of products and services may help you identify these groups.
- Customers by language.
- Customers by patterns of use, such as daily users, weekly users, infrequent users.

Organization: Crandall Public Library

System Name: The Building

Mission: To supply a safe, clean, comfortable, accessible, and efficient building for staff and public

Vision: The library as a place is warm and welcoming, accessible, and easy to use and find things. All staff strive to maintain a tidy, organized, efficient building despite crowded conditions and a layout of 12 levels. All departments continue to de-clutter their areas in expectation of a building renovation to three levels. The library uses off-site storage for building items. Library users and staff expect continuous evaluation of building services. The staff adapts to fluctuating circumstances within the library building's environment.

Team: Christine McDonald and Kathy Naftaly

Revision Date: January 6, 2004

Values:

Accommodation. We aspire to a building that is safe, clean, comfortable, and efficient in all systems for staff and patrons alike.

Teaming. The building team communicates and works together toward common goals.

Continuous Improvement. The building team actively evaluates and measures progress towards our mission.

Accommodation. When issues are discussed, the building team listens to every opinion and comes to consensus together.

Creativity. Problem solving is a creative process when new ideas are tried.

Measures (to be determined)

Feedback: Monthly Building Report, Monthly Roof Report, Service Contracts. Custodians. Cleaner. Head Custodian

Feedback: Board comments, suggestion box comments, phone calls, media reports, bldg. maintenance, forms

Suppliers: TBS for controls (AC), Monroe for boiler/ plumbing, GF, City workers, Boiler specialist, Alarm/ Security specialist, Fire Dept., Police Dept., Waste Mgmt., Dean Electric, Civil Service, Friends

Inputs: Chairs, tables, AV carts, ice melt, shovels, cleaning products (e.g. mops) toilet tissue, tool box, ladder, many sizes light bulbs, book carts, rain coats, gloves, plastic bags, plastic gloves, face masks, caution tape, wastebaskets, dumpster, telephone, computer

Primary Processes: Clean; setup; breakdown; change bulbs; arrange books at book sale and other events; coordinate with vendors, Friends, staff, customers; change paper/towels; mop; wash-windows, PCs, surfaces; paint; shovel; open and close building; set alarm; call vendors, Fire Dept., etc.; make minor repairs: empty wastebaskets; vacuum; dust; move; put up caution tape; intervene in case of security problems; re-start boiler; check boiler controls; check AC controls; store furniture; interact with staff and patrons; develop knowledge of staff duties to direct patrons; buy service contracts on all systems

Supporting Processes
Train staff in specific cleaning needs; purchase supplies; plan maintenance, provide in-service training

Outputs: Clean, ice-free sidewalks, snow removal and maintenance; emptied wastebaskets; filled paper product holders; comfortable climate in all seasons; organized book sales; predictable climate; optimal lighting; reasonable time for repairs; safe building; emptied book drop; well organized space; timely setup and breakdown of furniture; AV setup; screen setup; safe from hazardous materials

Customers
All staff
Local media
All patrons
City park workers

Figure 1-5 Facilities system map of Crandall Public Library.

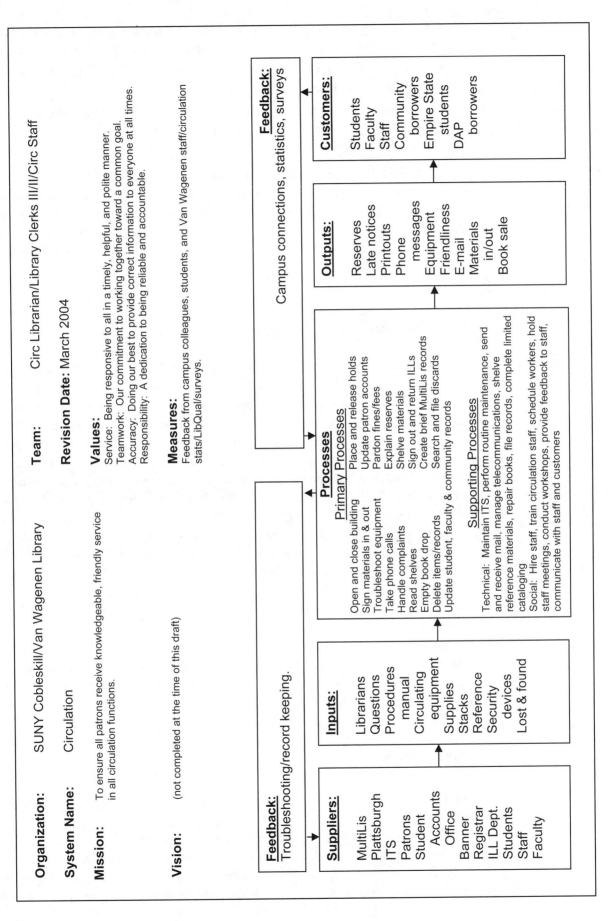

Organization: SUNY Cobleskill/Van Wagenen Library

System Name: Circulation

Mission: To ensure all patrons receive knowledgeable, friendly service in all circulation functions.

Vision: (not completed at the time of this draft)

Team: Circ Librarian/Library Clerks III/II/II/Circ Staff

Revision Date: March 2004

Values:
Service: Being responsive to all in a timely, helpful, and polite manner.
Teamwork: Our commitment to working together toward a common goal.
Accuracy: Doing our best to provide correct information to everyone at all times.
Responsibility: A dedication to being reliable and accountable.

Measures:
Feedback from campus colleagues, students, and Van Wagenen staff/circulation stats/LibQual/surveys.

Feedback: Troubleshooting/record keeping.

Feedback: Campus connections, statistics, surveys

Suppliers:
MultiLis
Plattsburgh
ITS
Patrons
Student
  Accounts
  Office
Banner
Registrar
ILL Dept.
Students
Staff
Faculty

Inputs:
Librarians
Questions
Procedures
  manual
Circulating
  equipment
Supplies
Stacks
Reference
Security
  devices
Lost & found

Processes

Primary Processes
Open and close building   Place and release holds
Sign materials in & out   Update patron accounts
Troubleshoot equipment   Pardon fines/fees
Take phone calls   Explain reserves
Handle complaints   Shelve materials
Read shelves   Sign out and return ILLs
Empty book drop   Create brief MultiLis records
Delete items/records   Search and file discards
Update student, faculty & community records

Supporting Processes
Technical: Maintain ITS, perform routine maintenance, send and receive mail, manage telecommunications, shelve reference materials, repair books, file records, complete limited cataloging
Social: Hire staff, train circulation staff, schedule workers, hold staff meetings, conduct workshops, provide feedback to staff, communicate with staff and customers

Outputs:
Reserves
Late notices
Printouts
Phone
  messages
Equipment
Friendliness
E-mail
Materials
  in/out
Book sale

Customers:
Students
Faculty
Staff
Community
  borrowers
Empire State
  students
DAP
  borrowers

Figure 1-6 Circulation system map of the SUNY–Cobleskill Van Wagenen Library.

- Customers who you don't see in the library, for example, phone callers, database users, Web surfers, people who send a friend or relative to the library for them.

- Customers in other libraries or outside your primary service area, including interlibrary loan users and chat reference users.

- Those who are not customers at all, those who never use the library or haven't used it for a long time. You might divide these into two groups—"potential customers" and "lapsed customers"—as many businesses do.

The three sample system maps provide some ideas for listing customers. The Pace University Library (figure 1-4) began with "students" and then realized that there were actually several different types of students, so they listed them—undergraduate, graduate, distance education, and so on. For the Crandall Public Library's facility system (figure 1-5) and SUNY–Cobleskill Library (figure 1-6), there are internal customers—staff—as well as external customers.

Step 1.5
Document feedback within the system.

The system map includes two boxes labeled "feedback," one with arrows leading from customers to the library process box and one with arrows from the process box back to suppliers. What channels does the library have to receive feedback from customers? Examples might include comment cards, public input at board meetings, surveys, focus groups, or other opportunities for the library to listen to customers. Remember that the arrow goes from the customer to the library and not the other way. Posters, newsletters, and other library publicity do not count as feedback. Chapter 4 includes some examples of customer feedback and ways to gather and analyze it. In figure 1-4, the Pace University Library included LibQUAL+, suggestion boxes, and preinstruction and postinstruction assessment in their thorough list of customer feedback sources.

The second feedback loop is from library processes to suppliers. Contracts and orders are two forms of feedback. Another less common one is the library sharing data about the performance of a vendor's product or service with the vendor. Crandall Public Library's list of feedback sources from processes to suppliers (figure 1-5) includes a monthly roof report and service contracts as well as informal reports from custodians.

Identifying inputs and suppliers, outputs and customers, and feedback loops can be enlightening. You will be surprised at how exciting the conversation among members of a library staff team can be. As the team shares its system map with others in the library, more and more detail about the library's system is added.

CONCLUSION

The library is a system with an important aim, usually expressed as a mission, vision, values, and measures.

The library system receives inputs from its suppliers and transforms them, through its processes, into outputs, which are focused on pleasing its customers. Customers provide feedback to the library system on its performance. Similarly, the library system provides feedback to its suppliers. A system map is a useful tool for describing the library system.

The quality of the system results from the interactions among its parts. These interactions—and not the people—are responsible for the overwhelming majority of the results of the system.

The system can be improved by improving the processes and the interactions among them. Reducing variation, improving upstream processes, ending inspection, and investing in the people in the system are powerful strategies for improvement.

Some of these statements seem boringly obvious; others conflict with common library practices and may stretch your comprehension. Suffice it to say that, for more than fifty years since Deming first articulated them, they have generated discussion around the world. We hope that you return to this section after you learn more about process improvement in general and study your own processes—and see if they make more sense to you then.

In chapter 2 we move inside the library process box to take a closer look at the processes—where the library takes the inputs, the raw materials, it receives and turns them into the products and services it produces for customers.

NOTES

1. The Baldrige Award for business, health care, and education incorporates the principles of quality improvement; see http://www.quality.nist.gov. The Six Sigma methodology, introduced at Motorola in the mid-1980s, uses the statistical methods pioneered by Deming and others to reduce variation.

2. William Scherkenbach, a Deming disciple, put together the idea of mission, vision, values, and measures as the Constancy of Purpose; see Scherkenbach (1995).

3. For a basic explanation of outcome-based evaluation, see, e.g., McNamara (1997). For additional resources about outcomes-based evaluation, visit http://national.unitedway.org/outcomes/library/pgmomres.cfm. For library-specific information about outcomes-based evaluation, see Durrance and Fisher (2005), Hernon and Dugan (2002), or IMLS (1999). For more information about the Balanced Scorecard evaluation framework, visit http://www.balancedscorecard.org.

4. The system map was invented by Tim Baer, QualStat Services, Indianapolis, Indiana.

5. For a good discussion of the reasons for using the term "customer" rather than "patron," "user," or "client," see Hernon and Altman (1998, 3–6).

Chapter 2 | Identify Library Processes and Assess Their Importance and Condition

In the system map you created in chapter 1, the center box is labeled "processes." This is where the work of the library takes place, as it transforms the inputs it receives from suppliers into the outputs it delivers to its customers. The transformation occurs through many processes. Let's take a closer look by defining *process*, listing all library processes within the system, identifying key processes, and selecting key processes to standardize and improve.

WHAT IS A PROCESS?

In library lingo, the word *process* has been used in the past in the context of "processing an item for circulation," meaning adding the labels, the book jacket, and the barcode. In the continuous improvement world, *process* has another and very specific meaning, which takes a little getting used to at first.

In figure 2-1, a *task* is a single action. A *process* is a series of interrelated tasks that convert inputs into outputs. A *system* is a series of interrelated processes.

Think about the process of making a cup of tea. The first task is to carry the teakettle to the sink. Second, turn on the faucet. Third, fill the teakettle. The fourth is to carry it to the stove and the fifth, to put it on the burner. Sixth, turn on the burner. Seventh, get a clean cup from the cupboard. Eighth, get a tea bag from the box. Ninth, put it into the cup. Tenth, wait until the water is boiling. Eleventh, pour boiling water over the tea bag in the cup. Twelfth, steep for three minutes.

The twelve tasks taken together are a single process, "make tea." The system in this case might be "serving breakfast," and other interrelated processes in the system might include squeezing fresh orange juice, making oatmeal, setting the table, and cleaning up after breakfast. The boundaries of the individual processes and the system are somewhat arbitrary; they can be set wherever it makes sense.

Step 2.1
List library processes.

One of the first challenges for the library planning to embark on continuous improvement is to identify all the processes included in its system. For most, this means thinking about all the clusters of tasks that the library does, across all its departments and locations and over time. In the traditional language of libraries, processes are different from departments, so simply listing "reference" or "children's services" doesn't suffice. Processes

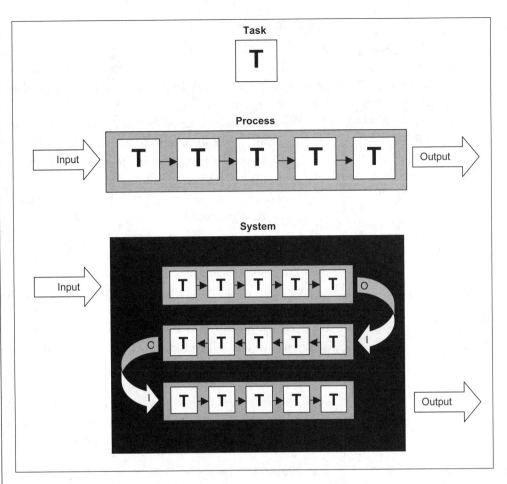

Figure 2-1 Processes are made up of interrelated tasks (T). Every process has at least one input and at least one output. Systems are made up of groups of interrelated processes; systems also have inputs and outputs.

most closely resemble traditional procedures—detailed, task-by-task descriptions of how to do something. In fact, processes are probably best understood as procedures-plus, procedures to which an understanding of suppliers, inputs, outputs, and customers has been added.

Appendix A is a comprehensive list of library processes, generated by several different libraries. Notice that you can identify processes broadly or in more detail. Many libraries start at the broader level, in order to get an overall view of their processes. When a library team really starts working on standardizing and improving the process, we have found that it usually subdivides the broad processes (subsystems) into several smaller pieces.

At the Vigo County Public Library, for example, the team decided to work on the process "select books." At their first meeting the team realized that this was too large and decided to break it into "select adult fiction," "select adult nonfiction," "select children's books," and "select gift books." As they began to work on "select gift books," they decided to focus on the books that were donated through the book return and at the desk, setting aside "select memorial books" and "select grant-funded books" for later.

Some library teams, on the other hand, may choose to start by listing the processes within a single department or service cluster. Let's consider two cases, reference and circulation:

The Reference System

If we think about "reference," we begin to realize that there are many different processes involved, from maintaining the print reference collection and renewing online databases to answering questions at the desk and on the phone and scheduling staff. But that is only the tip of the iceberg.

Think about renewing online databases. Renewing an online database subscription requires inputs in the form of information from suppliers including vendors, public services librarians, and ideally patrons. The process has outputs for customers, too—easy-to-access information for patrons and up-to-date information from the database for public service librarians, easy installation for IT staff, and timely and accurate invoicing for the purchasing department.

There are several tasks in the process, and it seems likely that those tasks will cross departmental boundaries, with public service librarians helping decide to renew or end the subscription, technical services staff maintaining the catalog records, IT staff managing technical details, purchasing staff placing the renewal and paying the bill. The public relations department may need to know about the renewal in order to promote use of the database. A misstep in any one of these process tasks could create mistakes or cause additional work in other tasks, either within this process or later when the results become the inputs for the next process.

And when we further realize how many locations and individuals are involved in answering reference questions—at the information desk, on the phone, in the branches, in each department, over all the hours the library is open, and maybe even through chat reference when it is not—it's not surprising that sometimes things go wrong.

The Circulation System

The list of forty-nine processes in figure 2-2 was created by several circulation teams participating in continuous improvement training. The teams spent no more than half an hour brainstorming this list, an activity which, in itself, made them realize that their processes were critically important and their jobs more complex than they had realized.

Notice that each process designation begins with a verb. As the Michigan City staff began to work on their processes, they discovered that many of the processes on their initial list were still too large to be considered one process. The process "Issue new library cards," for example, became "Issue new Michigan City resident cards," "Issue out-of-district cards," and "Issue out-of-state cards."

It is amazing how many processes a library—or even a department—has and how interconnected and interdependent they are. No wonder things sometimes go awry.

Primary and Supporting Processes

Processes are normally grouped into two categories—primary and supporting. Primary processes are those that directly affect customers. If one of the following primary processes was not done on any given day, customers would notice:

- open the library
- register new users
- present programs
- circulate materials

Issue a library card	Generate reports and statistics	Pull shelf holds
Check out books	Assist at self-check station	Open and close library
Check in books	Handle complaints	Check out AV equipment
Discharge items	Answer phone	Interview and hire new employees
Collect fines	Answer directional questions	Maintain and order supplies
Take patron requests	Answer simple item inquiries	Train new employees
Sort items for shelving	Handle damaged and lost items	Orient new employees
Update patron cards	Empty drop box	Sell PLAC & out-of-state cards
Send overdue notices	Clean dirty items	Collect people count and circulation count
Issue local card to PLAC customer	Send and receive faxes	
Perform community outreach	Assist patrons with copier	Inspect meeting room
Declare claims returned	Repair video	Set up meeting room
Renew items	Collect for damaged and lost items	Sort Friends donations
Place item on reserve	Refund lost payments	Handle Friends books
Cancel reserve	Shelve items	Collect Friends donations to book sale
Read shelves	Release from collection agency list	
Identify missing parts of items	Submit delinquent patron information to collection agency	Handle lost & found

Figure 2-2 Circulation processes.

- answer the phone
- close the library

Supporting processes, on the other hand, are those with only an indirect impact on customers. These might not be noticed if they weren't done for a while:

- hire staff
- orient staff
- evaluate staff
- hold board meetings
- plan for the future
- update the website
- pay bills
- change filters in the air conditioning units
- change light bulbs
- install computer software updates

Step 2.2
Identify key processes.

So many processes, so little time. After the library has developed a list of all its processes (perhaps using appendix A as a starting point), the next step is to identify which of those dozens—perhaps hundreds—of processes are most important for carrying out the library's mission, reaching its vision, and staying true to its values. No library has the resources to work on all its processes at once; choosing a few on which to focus is the next step. The library must answer two questions:

- Which processes are most important to achieving our goals?
- What is the current condition of these key processes?

There are both formal and informal ways to select a few processes upon which to focus. If you already know which processes need improvement, or you cannot work on the processes identified in the formal approach, use the following "Quick Shortcut for Selecting a Process." The more complete, formal approach is described in "Comprehensive Approach."

Quick Shortcut for Selecting a Process

Sometimes the library may decide which processes to improve through informal methods. Perhaps customers or staff members are complaining about a particular process. A public library with which we worked chose to work on their process "Sign up for a public access computer" because both customers and staff were complaining about the current process. An academic library chose "Renew database licenses" because, every year when renewals came up, they had forgotten what they did the year before, and they frequently failed to get all the input and approvals needed in a timely manner. For these two libraries it was quite obvious which processes needed improvement; they didn't need special research tools to figure it out.

Comprehensive Approach: Evaluating the Importance of Processes for Achieving Key Success Factors

The first step in identifying key processes is to evaluate the impact of every process on achieving the library's strategic goals and objectives, called here "key success factors."[1] To assist in this assessment, we have developed the Key Success Factors/Key Processes matrix (KSF/KP matrix), a simple visual tool that allows a group to reach consensus on the importance and condition of processes.

Step 2.2.1 *List processes in matrix.*

Using the list of processes you developed for your system—whether your system is the entire library or just a department or function, whether it is made up of broad or more detailed processes—write each process in the left-hand column of the matrix (figure 2-3). For the sake of brevity, we have used only some of the processes from the list in figure 2-2. In your actual use of the matrix, include all the processes in your system, at least at the "macro" level.

Step 2.2.2 *List key success factors in matrix.*

Identify the library's key success factors and write them across the top of the matrix. In this book we do not include a methodology for arriving at key success factors, since many valid approaches are already available in the library, business, and community development literature (Nelson 2001). Common to all strategic planning approaches is the

Key Success Factor A: Increase the use of library services by teens.
Key Success Factor B: Position the library as a technology leader in the community.
Key Success Factor C: Champion reading and literacy.
Key Success Factor D: Diversify funding for the library.

Process, Product, or Service	Key Success Factors				Importance add (A+B+C+D)	Condition
	A	B	C	D		
1. Select books						
2. Answer the phone						
3. Open the library						
4. Empty the book drop						
5. Hire staff						
6. Train and develop staff						
7. Plan programs						
8. Clean the library						
9. Select databases						
10. Maintain the shelf list						
11. Register new customers						
12. Create promotional strategies						
13. Send e-mail renewal reminders						
14. Conduct focus groups						
15. Hold board meetings						
16. Create the annual budget						
17. Update the website						
18. Pay bills						
19. Check out materials						
20. Install software updates						
TOTALS						

Importance: Assign points by considering how important each process is to achieving each key success factor:

> 5 = Process is very important to achieving the key success factor.
> 3 = Process is somewhat important to achieving the key success factor.
> 1 = Process may have minor impact on achieving key success factor.
> 0 = Process has no impact on key success factor.

Condition: Assign points based on the current condition of the process:

> 5 = Very good; this process delights customers.
> 4 = Good; this process usually works fine for customers and staff.
> 3 = Fair; occasional complaints indicate this process could use some improvement.
> 2 = Poor; this process sometimes causes problems for customers and staff.
> 1 = Very poor; this process frequently causes problems for customers and staff.

Figure 2-3   Key success factor/key process matrix, with processes.

assumption that the organization will choose a small number of goals, objectives, or strategic directions to form the focus of its efforts over the next planning period, ideally a year. It is this small number that we define as the key success factors. If your library does not have a formal strategic plan, you undoubtedly have a mental "to do" list for the next year or two. Write it down, share it with some others in your organization informally, and modify it according to their responses until you have arrived at a few areas of library focus—that is, key success factors. If you know your customers and your policymakers well, you won't be far off, but you will want to start thinking about a way to gather customer feedback, assess trends in your community (whatever your community is), and agree upon and formally adopt some shared key success factors soon. Limit the number of key factors to three to five; otherwise the effort will be overwhelming and quickly lose focus.

In figure 2-3, for example, four key success factors were chosen by the library and inserted across the top of the KSF/KP matrix: (1) Increase the use of library services by teens; (2) Position the library as a technology leader in the community; (3) Champion reading and literacy; and (4) Diversify funding for the library.

Step 2.2.3   *Rate the importance of each process for each key success factor.*

Assess the importance of each process for accomplishing each key success factor. Starting with the first process, ask how important each process is to each key success factor. In answering, use the following ratings:

5 = This process is very important for accomplishing this key success factor.

3 = This process is somewhat important for accomplishing this key success factor.

1 = This process is marginally important for accomplishing this key success factor.

0 = This process will have no impact on accomplishing this key success factor.

(Use only these ratings, never a 4 or 2. The idea is to create a separation.)

In figure 2-4, for example, the first process is "Select books." You ask, how important is "Select books" for increasing teens' use of library services? You decide that it is somewhat important, so you agree on a rating of 3. Next you ask, how important is "Select books" for positioning the library as a technology leader? Notice that you're not assessing the *impact of technology* on improving your process for selecting books, but the other way round. Technology may improve the process for selecting books, but that's not the question here; in this instance you are assessing the importance of the process for selecting books on positioning the library as a technology leader. Not much, you decide. The library may purchase print materials about technology, so you rate it a 1.

Next, how important is "Select books" for championing reading and literacy? Very important, you decide, so this one gets a 5. Continue to ask the question for the first process and the fourth key success factor. In this example, you decide that selecting books has no impact on diversifying funding.

Now go to the second process, repeat the question for each key success factor, and assign points across the second row. Then do the same for each process and key success factor until every box in the matrix is filled.

When you get down to asking how important it is to "Register new customers" for increasing teens' use of library services, remember to base your answer on the importance of the registering process to increasing teens' use, and not the other way around.

Key Success Factor A: Increase the use of library services by teens.
Key Success Factor B: Position the library as a technology leader in the community.
Key Success Factor C: Champion reading and literacy.
Key Success Factor D: Diversify funding for the library.

Process, Product, or Service	Key Success Factors				Importance add (A+B+C+D)	Condition (Good=5, Poor=1)
	A	B	C	D		
1. Select books	3	1	5	0	9	
2. Answer the phone	1	0	1	0	2	
3. Open the library	1	1	3	0	5	
4. Empty the book drop	1	1	5	0	7	
5. Hire staff	1	5	3	0	9	
6. Train and develop staff	5	5	5	0	15	
7. Plan programs	5	5	5	1	16	
8. Clean the library	1	1	3	1	6	
9. Select databases	3	5	1	0	9	
10. Maintain the shelf list	0	0	0	0	0	
11. Register new customers	1	5	3	0	9	
12. Create promotional strategies	5	5	5	5	20	
13. Send e-mail renewal reminders	1	5	5	1	12	
14. Conduct focus groups	5	5	5	1	16	
15. Hold board meetings	1	1	1	1	4	
16. Create the annual budget	0	3	3	1	7	
17. Update the website	5	5	3	0	13	
18. Pay bills	0	0	1	0	1	
19. Check out materials	1	1	5	0	7	
20. Install software updates	1	5	3	0	9	
TOTALS	44	60	66	11		

Importance: Assign points by considering how important each process is to achieving each key success factor:

> 5 = Process is very important to achieving the key success factor.
> 3 = Process is somewhat important to achieving the key success factor.
> 1 = Process may have minor impact on achieving key success factor.
> 0 = Process has no impact on key success factor.

Condition: Assign points based on the current condition of the process:

> 5 = Very good; this process delights customers.
> 4 = Good; this process usually works fine for customers and staff.
> 3 = Fair; occasional complaints indicate this process could use some improvement.
> 2 = Poor; this process sometimes causes problems for customers and staff.
> 1 = Very poor; this process frequently causes problems for customers and staff.

Figure 2-4   Key success factor/key process matrix, with importance totals.

You can complete this exercise in a group or use an individual balloting process. Assigning the importance rating is a matter of opinion, and individuals may not agree. If you choose to do it as a group, be sure to remind the participants that it is the importance of the *processes* and not the *participants' work* that they are rating. Expect considerable discussion as the group decides how to differentiate between a 5 and a 3 rating, for example. The conversation itself is valuable, even if agreement is not quick or perfect, for it begins to engage the participants in thinking about the processes and their relation to the key success factors, often a new experience. After a while, the group usually gets into a rhythm and is able to agree quickly upon a rating for the importance of each process to each key success factor.

You may choose to do the exercise through balloting first, because it gives everyone a chance to assess the importance of the processes individually, is faster, and doesn't require a meeting. If you do, be sure to include clear directions and perhaps some group discussion to increase understanding before balloting. Expect a wider range of ratings, since balloting by e-mail or mail eliminates the opportunity for discussion and consensus building. Perhaps the ideal solution is to give the group the exercise and instructions, give the members time (during the meeting or before it) to arrive at their own assessment, then share all the individual assessments at a meeting and endeavor to reach agreement.

Many people can identify about three to eight different processes that they're a part of. Some managers will find that they work with a dozen or more processes.
—Dianne Galloway (1994, 9)

Step 2.2.4   Determine importance of each process.

Add across each row to create a total for each process and discuss the results. Which are the key processes? Are you surprised by any that were or were not on the list? The processes with the highest totals are key processes because they have the largest impact across all of your key success factors. Because you don't have limitless time or staff to dedicate to improving processes, initially you will want to select only a handful of processes on which to focus, probably five or fewer. How many and which ones you select will depend primarily on the ratings, the library's capacity for working on improving the processes, and your instinct. Is there a natural clustering in the totals, perhaps a top quarter and bottom quarter? What else do you notice? Your conversation about the importance ratings may reveal some additional insights.

In figure 2-4, for example, six processes had totals of 10 points or more, so we might decide that they are the key processes: "Create promotional strategies" (20 points), "Plan programs" (16), "Conduct focus groups" (16), "Train and develop staff" (15), "Update the website" (13), and "Send e-mail renewal reminders" (12).

Did any of the processes have a total of 0? These processes have no impact on any of the key success factors. They are candidates for reduction or elimination, unless there is some compelling reason to continue them. Perhaps they are required for compliance. Perhaps they are outmoded and are no longer adding value. It's worth investigating. In figure 2-4, there is one process—"Maintain the shelf list"—with a total of 0.

Step 2.2.5   Determine support for each key success factor.

Add down to total the ratings in each key success factor column and pause to study the results of the KSF/KP matrix with your group. The completed matrix is a rich source of information about the library's processes.

Which key success factors received the highest and lowest column totals? The totals offer a picture of the level of the library's process support for each key success factor. The key success factors with the highest column totals are those best supported by current processes. Where the totals are low, the matrix alerts the library that, unless it develops some processes in these areas, it is unlikely to make much progress.

In figure 2-4, for example, key success factor C (Champion reading and literacy) is the best supported, with 66 points. Nearly every process on the list has some impact on this key success factor. Key success factor B (Position the library as a technology leader) is a close second, with 60 points and many processes supporting it. Key success factor D (Diversify funding for the library) is least supported by the processes on the list; many of them rated 0 or 1, and only one process—"Create promotional strategies"—rated a 5. It is unlikely that the library will be able to accomplish this key success factor without creating some processes to support it. Key success factor A (Increase the use of library services by teens) is supported by several processes but is 22 points short of the leading key success factor, so it may be another area in which additional processes are needed.

Step 2.2.6   *Assess the condition of current processes.*

The next step is to reach a consensus on the current condition of each key process. Returning to the matrix, use the right-most column to assign a value from 1 to 5 for the current condition of the process:

> 5 = Very good; this process delights customers and/or staff.
>
> 4 = Good; this process usually works fine for customers and staff.
>
> 3 = Fair; occasional complaints indicate that this process could use some improvement.
>
> 2 = Poor; this process sometimes causes problems for customers and staff.
>
> 1 = Very poor; this process frequently causes problems for customers and staff.

Encourage everyone participating in the discussion to use the full range of ratings, from 5 to 1, in order to create the best separation among all the processes. It may be difficult for some to rate any process less than a perfect 5 for fear of offending the individuals who work in that process. Remind the group again that it is the condition of the *process* and not *their own or other individuals' work* that they are rating. Processes may be in poor

Key Success Factor A: Increase the use of library services by teens.
Key Success Factor B: Position the library as a technology leader in the community.
Key Success Factor C: Champion reading and literacy.
Key Success Factor D: Diversify funding for the library.

Process, Product, or Service	Key Success Factors				Importance add (A+B+C+D)	Condition (Good=5, Poor=1)
	A	B	C	D		
1. Select books	3	1	5	0	9	2
2. Answer the phone	1	0	1	0	2	2
3. Open the library	1	1	3	0	5	5
4. Empty the book drop	1	1	5	0	7	5
5. Hire staff	1	5	3	0	9	4
6. Train and develop staff	5	5	5	0	15	2
7. Plan programs	5	5	5	1	16	5
8. Clean the library	1	1	3	1	6	4
9. Select databases	3	5	1	0	9	1
10. Maintain the shelf list	0	0	0	0	0	3
11. Register new customers	1	5	3	0	9	5
12. Create promotional strategies	5	5	5	5	20	4
13. Send e-mail renewal reminders	1	5	5	1	12	2
14. Conduct focus groups	5	5	5	1	16	1
15. Hold board meetings	1	1	1	1	4	4
16. Create the annual budget	0	3	3	1	7	2
17. Update the website	5	5	3	0	13	3
18. Pay bills	0	0	1	0	1	5
19. Check out materials	1	1	5	0	7	5
20. Install software updates	1	5	3	0	9	3
TOTALS	44	60	66	11		

Importance: Assign points by considering how important each process is to achieving each key success factor:

   5 = Process is very important to achieving the key success factor.
   3 = Process is somewhat important to achieving the key success factor.
   1 = Process may have minor impact on achieving key success factor.
   0 = Process has no impact on key success factor.

Condition: Assign points based on the current condition of the process:

   5 = Very good; this process delights customers.
   4 = Good; this process usually works fine for customers and staff.
   3 = Fair; occasional complaints indicate this process could use some improvement.
   2 = Poor; this process sometimes causes problems for customers and staff.
   1 = Very poor; this process frequently causes problems for customers and staff.

Figure 2-5   Key success factor/key process matrix, with condition totals.

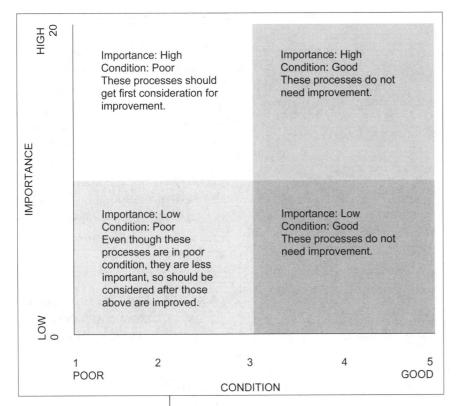

Figure 2-6 Scatter diagram template.

condition for many reasons, from outdated equipment to poor-quality inputs and many other factors, usually the result of the system and not the people in the system.

In figure 2-5, the participants reached a consensus on condition ratings for all twenty processes, using the full range from 1 through 5. They began, for example, with the first process and asked, in what condition is the "Select books" process? They pointed out that the process was slow and cumbersome for staff, who sometimes complained that they didn't know how other selectors were making decisions. They had also heard complaints from customers who didn't know what happened to their requests for purchase and who frequently used interlibrary loan when they found that the library did not own a recent title. Looking at the ratings, they decided this process rated a 2, since it sometimes caused problems for customers and staff.

If staff members are completing individual assessments of condition through balloting before the meeting, an average condition must be calculated. If condition assessment is done this way, the group may get a broader opinion of the condition but also lose the opportunity for rich discussion. A compromise might be to gather individual assessments of process condition from everyone and then have a representative group discuss the results.

Step 2.3
Select key processes to standardize and improve.

For a quick visual representation of the importance and condition of processes, create a scatter diagram. Begin by drawing a graph with an *x*- and *y*-axis, as in figure 2-6.

Step 2.3.1 *Set y-axis to establish range for importance scores.*

Number the *y*-axis from 0 to the largest possible total in the importance column. For example, in figure 2-5, values ranged from 0 to 20, so the *y*-axis in figure 2-6 extends from 0 to 20.

Step 2.3.2 *Set x-axis for condition ratings.*

Number the *x*-axis from 1 to 5 to cover the range of condition ratings.

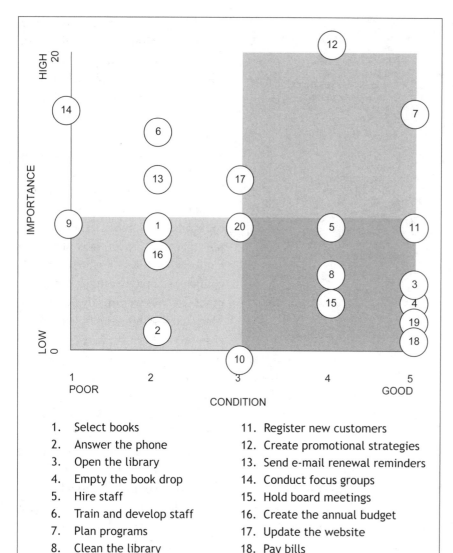

1. Select books
2. Answer the phone
3. Open the library
4. Empty the book drop
5. Hire staff
6. Train and develop staff
7. Plan programs
8. Clean the library
9. Select databases
10. Maintain the shelf list
11. Register new customers
12. Create promotional strategies
13. Send e-mail renewal reminders
14. Conduct focus groups
15. Hold board meetings
16. Create the annual budget
17. Update the website
18. Pay bills
19. Check out materials
20. Install software updates

Figure 2-7 Scatter diagram showing importance and condition of library key processes.

Step 2.3.3 *Plot process ratings.*

Using the first process on the first row of the KSF/KP matrix, go up the *y*-axis to its importance number, and then across to the corresponding condition number on the *x*-axis. Plot a point at that intersection and label it 1. See, for example, figure 2-7. Repeat for every pair of numbers, going up the *y*-axis for importance and across the *x*-axis for condition and labeling each with its number from the KSF/KP matrix.

Step 2.3.4 *Identify processes in most and least need of improvement.*

To select some processes on which to work, try dividing the scatter diagram into four areas, with roughly half the processes in the upper two quadrants and half the processes in the left-hand two quadrants. The areas may not necessarily be the same size. The purpose of this exercise is to identify a few important processes to improve, so choose those that have the highest importance and poorest condition. In figure 2-7, for example, the processes in the upper left area are very important and in poor condition. Three processes in this sector would be the logical focus for improvement efforts: (14) "Conduct focus groups," (6) "Train and develop staff," and (13) "Send e-mail renewal reminders." A fourth process—(9) "Select databases"—would also be a good process to improve, since it is in very poor condition and fairly important. A fifth one—(1) "Select books"—is also important and in moderately poor condition, so it would be a good candidate for improvement as well.

The points in the lower left quadrant are those processes that are in poor condition but less important. These would be the second choice for attention, since improving them would also have some impact. Sometimes a library may choose to focus on one of these because the more important processes are not approachable at the present time. In figure 2-7, four processes are in this area—(16) "Create the annual budget," (2) "Answer the phone," (20) "Install software updates," and (10) "Maintain the shelf list." Although they are in poor condition, they are not as important for accomplishing the key success factors.

The points in the upper and lower right quadrants represent processes that are in good condition and are more important or less important. These processes can be left alone.

Rating processes by importance and condition in reference to the library's key success factors is one way to reduce the lengthy list of processes to a manageable size. The discussion generated during the rating exercise is also valuable, since it engages the people who do the work in thinking about processes and their condition. The scatter diagram represents the importance and condition of processes visually, so that a group can see and discuss their choice of processes to improve.

Examples of Choosing Key Processes to Improve

Two examples illustrate the power of completing the KSF/KP matrix.

Mishawaka-Penn-Harris Public Library

Mishawaka-Penn-Harris Public Library planned to begin a library-wide initiative during which it would train six staff teams in process mastering and improvement. The assistant director sent us a list of twelve processes to be considered for improvement. We wondered how she had arrived at the processes listed and how they related to the library's overall directions.

We discovered that the library's existing long-range plan did not include key success factors, so we met with the director, assistant director, and human resources manager and asked what they were trying to accomplish in the next few years. After thoughtful discussion, they identified six areas of focus, which we used as the informal key success factors: (A) Take advantage of up-to-date technology in library services and operations; (B) Provide high-quality, efficient customer service; (C) Develop staff expertise in support of the library's mission; (D) Support internal and external communications that help the library understand and respond to customer needs; (E) Reexamine the role of reference service in the twenty-first century; and (F) Ensure the library's future financial security.

Next we used the KSF/KP matrix with the leadership team to rate the importance of the twelve processes (see figure 2-8). As we worked through this exercise, the leaders realized that some of the processes on their original list were not as important to the key success factors as other processes not on the list. By the time we were finished, we had added five more processes to the list, which certainly was still not comprehensive. Instead, the list was largely the result of complaints and issues that the leaders had noticed in the library. They didn't need to rate the condition of the processes, because they were problematic by definition.

The processes they picked are the six in bold in figure 2-8. Notice that they chose the four top-ranked processes ("Answer reference questions"; "Train staff on new software"; "Orient new staff"; and "Select young adult materials") but also two others that were not as highly ranked ("Prepare DVDs for circulation" and "Send fine notices"). Why? They needed to release twenty staff members from desk duty for the process improvement work, and choosing other more highly ranked processes would have created scheduling difficulties.

Working through the KSF/KP matrix had an added benefit. The leaders noticed that three of the key success factors were reasonably well supported by the processes on the list, whereas three others were not. Because the list of processes was not comprehensive, they agreed to think about these factors and try to identify processes in the library that

Key Success Factors

A. Take advantage of up-to-date technology in library services and operations.
B. Provide high-quality, efficient customer service.
C. Develop staff expertise in support of the library's mission.
D. Support internal and external communications that help the library understand and respond to customer needs.
E. Reexamine the role of reference service in the twenty-first century.
F. Ensure the library's future financial security.

Process	Key Success Factor						Importance (A+B+C...)
	A	B	C	D	E	F	
Order materials	0	0	0	3	5	3	11
Receive materials	0	0	0	3	5	2	10
Prepare DVDs for circulation	**0**	**0**	**0**	**3**	**5**	**2**	**10**
Weed materials	1	1	0	1	5	1	9
Select young adult materials	**1**	**0**	**1**	**3**	**5**	**5**	**15**
Check out materials	0	5	1	5	0	1	12
Check in materials	0	5	1	5	0	1	12
Shelve materials	0	3	1	5	5	1	15
Collect fines	0	3	0	5	0	1	9
Process new cards	0	5	0	5	0	0	10
Answer reference questions	**1**	**5**	**4**	**5**	**5**	**3**	**23**
Sign up for a computer	1	5	3	3	2	0	14
Train staff on new software	**3**	**5**	**5**	**5**	**5**	**0**	**23**
Create flyers	0	0	1	5	1	0	7
Proofread PR materials	0	0	0	5	0	0	5
Orient new staff	**0**	**5**	**5**	**5**	**4**	**1**	**20**
Send fine notices	**0**	**5**	**0**	**5**	**0**	**0**	**10**
TOTALS	7	47	22	61	47	21	

Importance: Assign points by considering how important each process is to achieving each key success factor:

5 = Process is very important to achieving the key success factor.
3 = Process is somewhat important to achieving the key success factor.
1 = Process may have minor impact on achieving key success factor.
0 = Process has no impact on key success factor.

Figure 2-8 Key success factor/key process matrix, Mishawaka-Penn-Harris Public Library.

INDIANA LIBRARY FEDERATION
CONSTANCY OF PURPOSE

MISSION

The mission of the Indiana Library Federation is to promote all libraries in Indiana and foster the professional growth of its members.

VISION

- **MEMBERSHIP** We are an organization of all eligible individuals and groups passionately committed to the power of libraries and librarians to improve the quality of life in Indiana communities.
- **COLLABORATION/PARTNERSHIPS** We effectively collaborate with all individuals and organizations to support and promote Indiana libraries.
- **TECHNOLOGY** We use the latest appropriate technologies to accomplish the ILF mission and goals.
- **PROFESSIONAL DEVELOPMENT** We provide and promote effective professional development for individuals and libraries.
- **PUBLIC RELATIONS/ADVOCACY** We influence policy. Citizens use, support, and fully fund all Indiana libraries. Decision makers seek out librarians as information providers.
- **SERVICES** We help local libraries improve their services to local residents.

VALUES

- **DEMOCRATIC IDEALS** All members have a voice and diversity is respected.
- **INTEGRITY** We speak the truth and honor our commitments.
- **RELATIONSHIPS** We support and encourage collegiality and collaborations.
- **EFFECTIVE** We focus on actions that efficiently further our mission and vision.

MEASURES

1. Members as a percentage of potential members
2. Member retention
3. Professional development: conference evaluations, attendance, follow-up survey
4. Promotion of libraries: advertising, invitations to join collaborations, web hits, grassroots contacts
5. Advocacy: legislative successes, local successes

Figure 2-9 Constancy of Purpose statement, Indiana Library Federation.

would support them. If, after looking around, they could not identify processes, or if the processes existed but were in poor condition, they would be able to target them for improvement. Unless they found or invented processes in these areas, they would not likely make much headway on those key success factors.

Indiana Library Federation

Identifying key processes and assessing their condition is a useful exercise in organizational contexts other than libraries. When the Indiana Library Federation (ILF) engaged in strategic planning, it conducted a survey of member priorities and completed an environmental scan. Next it agreed upon new, more concise mission, vision, values, and measures (figure 2-9).

From these it reached consensus on five key success factors: (1) Get, keep, and develop members, (2) Shape policy, (3) Evaluate the ILF organizational structure, (4) Improve communications, and (5) Develop and manage collaborations.

The strategic planning committee asked the staff to develop a list of all the ILF's processes (figure 2-10). The staff started to work and quickly decided they had to divide the list into staff processes, member volunteer processes (those for which the board, committees, associations, and other units were entirely responsible), and staff/volunteer processes in which both staff and members played a role. Not surprisingly, their list of office processes was more complete and detailed than the list of volunteer-driven processes. For example, "Recruit new members" had no subprocesses listed, whereas "Renew members" was described in some detail. In another example, the legislative advocacy work of ILF, one of its two

Process	Subprocess	Who Is Responsible s=staff, v=volunteer
Arrange unit library insurance	Compile underwriting application	s
Arrange unit library insurance	Process/follow up with institutions	s
Conduct strategic planning	Conduct strategic planning	sv
Develop members	Appoint members to committees	v
Develop policy	Communicate through listservs	v
Develop policy	Conduct and process evaluations	v
Develop policy	Hold board meetings	v
Develop policy	Hold committee meetings	v
Elect volunteer leaders	Announce election results in publications	sv
Elect volunteer leaders	Mail ballots to members	sv
Elect volunteer leaders	Prepare biographical information for publication	sv
Elect volunteer leaders	Receive and process ballots	sv
Elect volunteer leaders	Recognize new officers at annual business meeting	sv
Elect volunteer leaders	Send letters to nominees and winners	sv
Elect volunteer leaders	Solicit nominations	sv
Handle money	Compile monthly reports for accountant	s
Handle money	Create invoices	s
Handle money	Deposit money in bank	s
Handle money	Generate deposit reports	s
Handle money	Generate financial reports for units	s
Handle money	Maintain investment records	s
Handle money	Pay bills	s
Handle money	Process checks and credit card payments	s
Handle money	Process payroll	s
Handle money	Reconcile bank accounts	s
Manage AIME Media Fair	Design and produce award plaques	sv
Manage AIME Media Fair	Process registrations (and money)	sv
Manage AIME Read Aloud project	Manage AIME Read Aloud project	s
Manage Young Hoosier Book Award	Design YHBA and Rosie materials	sv
Manage Young Hoosier Book Award	Develop YHBA and Rosie lists	sv
Manage Young Hoosier Book Award	Fill orders for YHBA and Rosie materials	sv
Manage Young Hoosier Book Award	Process YHBA and Rosie registrations	sv
Manage Young Hoosier Book Award	Reorder YHBA and Rosie materials	sv
Manage conferences	Coordinate exhibit show	sv
Manage conferences	Design conference theme and logo	sv
Manage conferences	Design products for conference store	sv
Manage conferences	Develop and design conference program book	sv
Manage conferences	Develop and design conference brochure	sv
Manage conferences	Print and distribute conference brochure	sv
Manage conferences	Do public relations for conferences	sv

Figure 2-10 List of processes, Indiana Library Federation.

Process	Subprocess	Who Is Responsible s=staff, v=volunteer
Manage conferences	Enter conference registration data	sv
Manage conferences	Generate reports for unit after conference	sv
Manage conferences	Order materials for conference store	sv
Manage conferences	Prepare registration materials (nametags, meal tickets)	sv
Manage conferences	Process evaluations from conference	sv
Manage conferences	Produce reports from database	sv
Manage conferences	Update member database with changes	sv
Manage electronic communications	Manage Web site	s
Manage electronic communications	Manage Bravelo	s
Manage electronic communications	Send and receive e-mail	s
Manage electronic communications	Send and receive faxes	s
Manage mailings	Deliver mailings to post office/mailing house	s
Manage mailings	Design and print mailings	s
Manage mailings	Maintain postage meter	s
Manage mailings	Prepare mailings (stuff envelopes)	s
Manage mailings	Process WHEELS mailings	s
Manage mailings	Provide mailing list to ILF and external customers	s
Manage office	Answer phones	s
Manage office	File materials	s
Manage office	Open and distribute mail	s
Manage public relations projects	Complete monthly grant reports	sv
Manage public relations projects	Design public awareness products	sv
Manage public relations projects	Develop public awareness campaign theme	sv
Manage public relations projects	Work with legislative advocates	sv
Manage public relations projects	Provide public relations	sv
Manage volunteer leadership	Invent ideas for conferences/special projects	v
Manage volunteer leadership	Hold leadership retreat for unit leaders	s
Manage volunteer leadership	Hold meeting for district chairs	s
Manage volunteer leadership	Manage large-scale mailings	s
Manage volunteer leadership	Produce and edit leadership notebook	s
Manage volunteer leadership	Provide budgeting guidance	s
Manage volunteer leadership	Schedule meeting rooms	s
Manage volunteer leadership	Hold committee meetings	s
Produce publications	Collect content for publications	sv
Produce publications	Coordinate job listings with Indiana State Library	sv
Produce publications	Design layout of collateral materials	sv
Produce publications	Design layout of publication	sv
Produce publications	Edit content for publications	sv
Produce publications	Invoice advertisers	sv
Produce publications	Receive and process subscriptions	sv

Process	Subprocess	Who Is Responsible s=staff, v=volunteer
Produce publications	Solicit advertising for publications	sv
Produce publications	Write and distribute press releases	sv
Recruit new members	Do public relations to solicit members	v
Renew members	Enter data for membership	s
Renew members	Manage online membership renewal	s
Renew members	Produce and mail membership cards/packets	s
Renew members	Produce reports from database	s
Renew members	Update member database with changes	s

Figure 2-10   List of processes, Indiana Library Federation (cont.).

missions, which is supported by an active volunteer committee and a contract with a lobbying firm, was represented on the list by one subprocess under "Manage public relations projects." Missing from the process list were the processes for hiring/reviewing the lobbying firm, developing the federation's legislative platform, and communicating with the lobbying firm and with members. The list also revealed some redundancy. For example, the subprocess "Deposit money in bank" appeared under more than one process. The staff talked about this redundancy and decided that, because this process was the same or similar regardless of the project, it could be listed just once.

Next, the strategic planning committee members completed the KSF/KP matrix, using the larger processes rather than the subprocesses. Using these broad processes was perhaps not ideal; committee members had a tough time making a judgment about importance and condition. If time and other circumstances allow it, it is usually better to use the full, detailed list of subprocesses. When the ILF committee added the columns, it was startled to learn that some key success factors were supported by fewer processes than others, as shown in figure 2-11. The most processes were in place for success factor A (Get, keep, and develop members) and the fewest for factors B and C (Shape policy, and Evaluate the ILF organizational structure).

Adding the totals across, they found the processes most important to supporting the five key success factors to be (14) "Manage volunteer leadership"; (7) "Maintain electronic communications"; (12) "Manage the office"; (15) "Produce publications"; and (13) "Manage public awareness projects."

With some difficulty, they assigned a rating for the condition of each of the broad processes. As they looked at the condition totals in each row, their biggest "a-ha" was that the office processes were in good condition (e.g., "Handle money," "Manage conferences," "Manage mailings," and "Manage the office") while some member-driven processes were in poor condition. In the first key success factor area—Get, keep, and develop members—the committee saw that the staff process of renewing members was in reasonably good condition. On the other hand, the processes "Recruit new members" and "Develop members" were not in such good condition. Perhaps the lack of detail in the process list is related to the poor condition of the process, they mused.

Since then, the membership committee has discovered that every district had a volunteer membership chair with a job description, but that these volunteers were unaware

Key Success Factor A: Get, keep, and develop members.
Key Success Factor B: Shape policy.
Key Success Factor C: Evaluate the ILF organizational structure.
Key Success Factor D: Improve communications.
Key Success Factor E: Develop and manage collaborations.

Process, Product, or Service	Key Success Factors					Importance add (A+B+C+D+E)	Condition (Good=5, Poor=1)
	A	B	C	D	E		
1. Arrange unit library insurance	3	0	0	0	1	4	5
2. Conduct strategic planning	5	3	3	3	1	15	2
3. Develop members	5	3	3	3	3	17	3
4. Develop policy	3	1	1	3	1	9	4
5. Elect volunteer leaders	5	3	3	3	3	17	3
6. Handle money	1	0	1	0	0	2	5
7. Maintain electronic communications	5	5	3	5	5	23	2
8. Manage AIME Media Fair	3	0	0	3	1	7	4
9. Manage Young Hoosier Bk Award	3	0	0	3	1	7	5
10. Manage conferences	5	1	1	5	3	15	5
11. Manage mailings	5	1	1	5	1	13	5
12. Manage office	5	3	5	5	5	23	5
13. Manage public awareness projects	3	5	0	5	5	18	4
14. Manage volunteer leadership	5	5	5	5	5	25	2
15. Produce publications	5	3	3	5	3	19	3
16. Recruit new members	5	3	1	3	5	17	1
17. Renew current members	5	3	1	3	3	15	4
TOTALS	71	39	31	59	46		

Importance: Assign points by considering how important each process is to achieving each key success factor:

    5 = Process is very important to achieving the key success factor.

    3 = Process is somewhat important to achieving the key success factor.

    1 = Process may have minor impact on achieving key success factor.

    0 = Process has no impact on key success factor.

Condition: Assign points based on the current condition of the process:

    5 = Very good; this process delights customers.

    4 = Good; this process usually works fine for customers and staff.

    3 = Fair; occasional complaints indicate this process could use some improvement.

    2 = Poor; this process sometimes causes problems for customers and staff.

    1 = Very poor; this process frequently causes problems for customers and staff.

Figure 2-11   Key success factor/key process matrix, Indiana Library Federation.

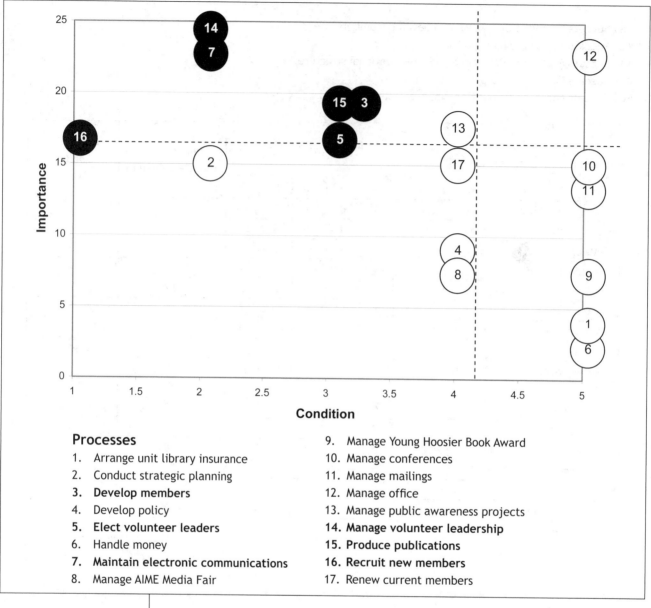

Processes

1. Arrange unit library insurance
2. Conduct strategic planning
3. **Develop members**
4. Develop policy
5. **Elect volunteer leaders**
6. Handle money
7. **Maintain electronic communications**
8. Manage AIME Media Fair
9. Manage Young Hoosier Book Award
10. Manage conferences
11. Manage mailings
12. Manage office
13. Manage public awareness projects
14. **Manage volunteer leadership**
15. **Produce publications**
16. **Recruit new members**
17. Renew current members

Figure 2-12 Scatter diagram of key processes, Indiana Library Federation.

and unsupported in this work. The former structure of membership captains in the largest public and academic libraries had also fallen into disuse. While ILF works to reinvigorate these processes, they are also working on new ways to involve members in the work and network of ILF.

Finally, the planning committee plotted the importance and condition of ILF processes on a scatter diagram (see figure 2-12), which revealed the processes that were important but not in good condition: (16) "Recruit new members," (14) "Manage volunteer leadership," (7) "Maintain electronic communications," (15) "Produce publications," (3) "Develop members," and (5) "Elect volunteer leaders." As this book goes to press, ILF has begun work on improving most of these processes.

CONCLUSION

A series of interrelated tasks is a process; a series of interrelated processes forms the library system, which may encompass the whole library or a department, branch, or other subsystem of the library.

Primary processes in the library are those that directly impact customers. Supporting processes, which often are not visible to customers, provide the human and technical support for primary processes.

Among all the processes in the library, some are more important than others to accomplishing the library's key success factors. By assessing the importance and condition of these key processes, library staff can identify a few processes on which to focus improvement efforts. The KSF/KP matrix and scatter diagram are useful tools for assessing the importance and condition of library processes and visually representing the results.

After selecting a small number of processes that are key to achieving the library's vision and need improvement, the next step is to create a common understanding of the tasks in the process and how they benefit customers (internal as well as external). This exercise, called "process mastering," is completed by a team. As team members create process masters, they are in control and are learning about the process as they standardize it. In chapter 3 we describe how to standardize a process by creating a process master.

NOTE

1. Key success factors may also be called "goals," "strategic directions," "focus areas," or something similar. Whatever the term, these are the few absolutely essential tasks upon which the library must focus, during the planning period, in order to carry out its mission, reach its vision, and stay true to its values.

Chapter 3 | **Standardize the Process**

Standardizing a process is the first step in process improvement. Without a stable, known process situation, it is difficult to know if any change has really made the process better or worse. Thus, any attempt to improve a process without first standardizing it is most likely doomed to failure.

Process improvement expert Peter Scholtes makes a strong case for the benefits of standardizing processes:

> Repeatable tasks can be studied and improved. We can determine the most efficient, reliable, safest, and most productive way we know to do this work. Then we can document that method, teach it to everyone involved in the task and reinforce its continual use in a variety of worker-friendly ways. . . .
>
> Standardizing a task around a single best method results in a better product and service for customers, greater ease in training new workers, and improving ability to solve problems and improve the process even more. While the best known method is being used as part of the routine, employees can continue to study the task to come up with an even better method. The effort thus keeps going. (1998, 119)

Another process expert, Brian Joiner, agrees: "Training and standardization create a nice positive spiral. A high degree of standardization is needed to make training possible. Without standardization, training is cumbersome, inefficient, and generally ineffective. And without effective training, any standard is soon lost" (1994, 200).

In this chapter, we discuss how to form a team, think about customer and supplier needs, and standardize the tasks in a process.

The best way to standardize a process is to enlist a team of people who normally do the process—the real experts—to document the process using a prescribed series of steps designed to guide them to consider all aspects of the process. The result is a document called a "process master."[1] Components of a completed process master include a flowchart of the process, with key tasks noted; screens for internal and external customers and suppliers; key tasks worksheets; and a list of supplies or tools required to do the process.

Figure 3-1 shows a deployment flowchart of the participants and the tasks involved. A deployment flowchart is a visual representation of all the tasks in a process displayed in a manner that indicates who is responsible for the tasks and in what order they are accomplished. The people or positions listed across the top of the flowchart are referred to as the "cast of characters." Below them is a listing in sequence of all interrelated tasks directed at accomplishing the process.

The suggested cast of characters includes

Sponsor. The sponsor might be the director, department head, branch manager, or functional team leader—anyone with authority to form a team.

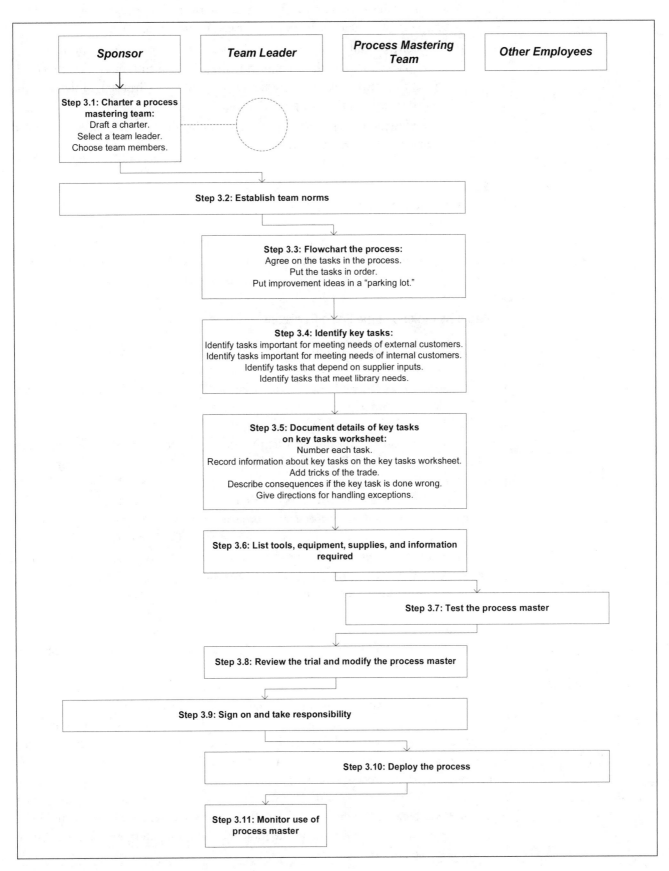

Figure 3-1 Deployment flowchart for creating a process master.

Team leader. This person acts as the convener for the process mastering team and is the point of contact between the sponsor and the process mastering team.

Process mastering team. The team typically includes people who work in the process every day, as well as perhaps suppliers to the process or customers of the process. If specific expertise is needed, an expert may be added to the team, or the expertise may be sought during the process mastering.

Other employees. Others play supporting roles, testing drafts of the process master and giving feedback and suggestions.

Step 3.1
Charter a process mastering team.

A sponsor who sees the need and has the authority initiates the process mastering work. Drafting a charter helps the sponsor clarify the task, specify final results, give necessary authority to the team, allay any concerns, and specify reporting procedures.

Begin by Making Some Basic Decisions

As the sponsor prepares to draft the charter, he/she answers the following questions:

What is the purpose or overall mission of the assignment? It is a good idea to document why a particular process has been chosen for standardization. As time passes, the sponsor, team leader, and team members may become caught up in the work of the moment and forget what prompted the standardization effort.

What is the name of the process? Many times people simply do things in their jobs without giving names to them. Naming the process forces them to define its limits and its purpose.

Where does the process begin and end? This sounds like a silly question, but sometimes the beginning and end of a process are not as clear-cut as participants might want to believe, since processes are interrelated, with one following immediately after another. Some hints for discerning the boundaries are physical (departments, rooms, materials, distance); some are less structured, such as networks, skills, timing, or size.

Processes are almost always larger than you think. Try to size processes so there are no more than fifty tasks.

Another issue that is important in sizing the process you plan to standardize is determining at what level of detail to work. The "right" level is what is required to accomplish standardization of the process. This is something learned from experience, but do not be surprised when processes almost always contain many more tasks than you anticipated.

Who are the people who work in the process? This issue involves simply thinking about who and how many people do, or are involved in doing, this process. For example, you might think about whether the people involved are full time or part time, new or experienced, positive or resistant, loners or team players. This is helpful when you consider the composition of the process mastering team.

Who is the process team leader? The supervisor of the area in which the process resides is a likely candidate to be the team leader. This is not a requirement, however, and there are sometimes good reasons to designate someone else who spends most of his/her time working in the process.

Our team is working really well together. We were not necessarily aware of the problems with our process.
—Miguelina Molina, Suffern (NY) Free Library

A Special Word about the Roles of Sponsors and Supervisors

Giving responsibility for standardizing and improving processes to a staff team is a new way of working for many libraries. Because it is new, everyone in the organization will have questions and concerns. One of the sponsor's most important responsibilities is to support and encourage the effort. In addition, the sponsor must demonstrate personal commitment to this new way of working. Among the sponsor's most important responsibilities are to use the language of continuous improvement, use process data in making decisions, allow time for teams to learn (even from their failures), help teams solve problems, and expect results.

If the supervisor of the process is not on the team, the sponsor must take special care to ensure that the supervisor is well informed about the process mastering charter, willing to accept the work of the chartered team, and able to provide support. Supervisors have suggested several practical ways to accomplish these objectives:

- Offer opportunities for supervisors to learn the theories, tools, and vocabulary themselves. Supervisors have processes, too, so it might be that they could choose a process and learn process mastering themselves before their staff members get involved.
- Communicate frequently. Make sure that supervisors receive a copy of the charter, team minutes, and any other reports the sponsor receives. Add informal communications to these formal channels.
- Be explicit about the support supervisors are expected to provide. Will they need to find time for their staff to meet? Will they need to provide a space? Will they need to answer questions from other staff? Will they need to provide encouragement to the team? Will they need to help the team resolve problems, if any occur?

Team Considerations

How many people are needed on the team? Teams generally work most effectively with a maximum of six members. More people on a team slows progress. Although process masters can be done by one person, it is best to involve several. The discussion during process mastering is one of the key strengths of this approach, for it allows people to get to know and better understand each other and to hear a variety of ideas and concerns— all directed at the process.

Should an outside expert be included on the team? Depending on the nature of the process, it may be helpful to include a person with specific expertise on the team. Processes in which safety, technical, personnel, or financial knowledge is essential are good examples.

Should a supplier or customer of the process be included on the team? Depending on the reason for mastering the process, it may be a good idea to include a customer of or supplier to the process. The customer brings a different perspective to what is really important in the process and how it might be standardized in a better way. The supplier can suggest different supplies or how to use the supplies effectively.

How is each shift or branch represented? If the process is to be truly standardized in an organization, it should include input from all involved in the process, regardless of their hours or where they work. Including representatives from all shifts and locations often influences when and where the team meetings can be held.

> *Preparing the instruction room was a big problem for us. The instruction librarians would find technology that didn't work, spilled sticky drinks, and missing supplies. None of them wanted to be responsible for the shared room. Midway through the process mastering, we realized that the departmental secretary was one of our suppliers and she could help us.*
>
> —Stephan J. Macaluso, Sojourner Truth Library, SUNY-New Paltz

Logistics

What day and time will the team meet? Mastering a single process takes six to ten hours, depending on the team's experience and the complexity of the process. It is best to have a standard time each week for the team to meet. Limiting meetings to two hours once a week allows sufficient time for active work and reflection and keeps team members focused. Note that processes can be mastered over a shorter period if standardization or timing are critical.

Team sponsors probably have a good idea when it is least disruptive for people to be away from their normal work, but whenever possible let the team make the final decision about when to meet.

Does the team need training in process mastering? This book is designed to provide sponsors, team leaders, and team members with everything they need to complete a process master. Some organizations hire a consultant to train selected employees to complete an initial process master. The trained employees are then able to lead teams themselves after they are chartered. Whether using the book or a consultant, the sponsor is important in providing support for team leaders as they learn by doing.

What resources (meeting space, supplies, time) are available? As the sponsor prepares to charter a process mastering team, he/she should anticipate the resources the team will need and plan accordingly. Typical supplies needed include 3- by 5-inch sticky notes, felt-tipped pens, a flipchart, and notebooks or file folders. Remember that meeting time is precious, so whenever possible have resources available when the meeting starts.

What is the target date for completion of the process master? With weekly two-hour meetings, it takes three to five weeks to complete a process master. If completion date is critical, the schedule of meetings may need to be adjusted.

Cautions

What circumstances or work products, if any, would cause the sponsor to reject the work of the team? This is where the sponsor should list any issues that might be of concern. One of the worst things that can happen to a process mastering team is for it to do its best work only to have the sponsor reject all or part of the results.

Might there be adverse effects on surrounding processes or customers if this process is standardized? At first thought, standardizing a process could only be good. It is not uncommon, however, for a seemingly innocent process standardization to have a negative effect on surrounding processes or even on customers. Likewise, sometimes standardizing a process puts new demands on supplying processes. The sponsor shouldn't become overly stressed about this issue, but some thought should be given to the possible ramifications of standardizing any process.

Are there additional worries that should be included in the charter? This is a final question to help the sponsor reflect on things that might happen if a process mastering team is chartered.

Step 3.1.1 *Draft the charter.*

After answering the questions just listed, the sponsor is ready to draft a team charter. The charter is a mini-contract that sets out in simple terms what is expected of the process mastering leader and team. Figure 3-2 shows a blank charter with notes.[2] Figures 3-3 and 3-4 are examples of completed team charters.

About this time you may be thinking, is it worth all this work just to initiate a process mastering team? After all, most library managers have created charges for and participated in committees and task forces for years. And yet . . . communication in all organizations continues to be an issue, so thoughtful consideration and putting into writing what is expected is definitely a good continuous improvement investment. The chartering process is different in several key ways from the usual committee charge:

- It serves as a discussion guide for the sponsor and team leader, giving them an opportunity to discuss and fine-tune the purpose, products, authority, limits, and reporting expectations for the team.

- It spells out clearly the team's authority, allowing them to operate independently.

- It spells out limits to their authority, to the extent that the sponsor can anticipate them, so the team also knows what it cannot do (or what it must not fail to do) without requesting specific permission.

- It defines the purpose, product, and timeframe, so that the sponsor, team leader, and all members know the expectations.

Date Number	(You will need this when you have several charters)
Charter	(Name of the charter)
To	(Team Leader) (Members, if known)
From	(Sponsor)
Purpose	A clear statement of the objectives.
Product/ expected results	Describe the specific outcomes that are desired.
Authorities	Use this area to describe or list authority that is being delegated for carrying out this project—money, time, space, contacts, travel, etc.
Limitations or boundaries	List worries or actions that are unacceptable in carrying out this project. Listing means or actions that are unacceptable frees the team to use any other methods or approaches to get the job done.
Reporting	Describe when, how often, in what form, and to whom reports or communication should be made about progress. Many times the phrase "or whenever the terms of the charter are violated" is used in this section.

Figure 3-2 Charter template.

Step 3.1.2 Select a team leader.

After the sponsor has considered the questions prior to drafting a charter, choosing a team leader should be fairly straightforward. In addition to considering the natural process leader and the supervisor, give consideration to individuals who

- have the respect of their peers and subordinates

- are comfortable being in front of a group

- are responsible

- can plan

- are mature and stable

- are knowledgeable about the process

- have team-leading skills

- are results driven

Leading a process mastering team is a growth experience.[3] After some experience as a team member, there is an opportunity to bring a promising employee along by putting him/her in charge of a team.

Date	October 28, 2004
Charter	Prepare library support for online learning
To	Continuous Assessment/Continuous Improvement Team (Shockey, Nichols, Parry, Shaffer)
From	Library Director (Bell)
Purpose	To prepare to integrate effective library presence in SUNY Oswego online courses
Product/ expected results	Tools, templates, and training for librarians
	Process master(s) for integration into online courses
	Outline of library content recommended as standard course information for courses using CourseSpace, SLN, and other online applications
	PR suggestions regarding library component of online courses
Authorities	To work with other librarians and faculty, especially instruction workgroup
	To work with CourseSpace steering committee and administrators
Limitations or boundaries	Don't fail to...
	Present RAPS to librarians on current online courseware by end of fall 2004
	Provide deployment and Gantt charts for development of products listed above by Dec. 2004
	Deliver completed products by June 15, 2004
	Have Mary Beth review all draft documents
Reporting	Report to instruction group
	Report to Mary Beth Bell at least monthly via e-mail

Figure 3-3 Charter, SUNY–Oswego Library.

Step 3.2
Establish team norms.

Step 3.1.3 Choose team members.

Next the sponsor meets with the chosen team leader to discuss the charter. They clear up any questions and adjust the charter accordingly. After considering such things as the number of team members required, representation from various locations and shifts, individuals' availability (existing workload, schedule, and vacations), and the communication skills, knowledge, and personalities needed, they generate a list of possible team members.

Communication skills and respect for fellow employees are two important attributes for team members, because they must convey information to and from process workers who are not on the team. The team members must share what is being decided in the team meetings and solicit feedback and suggestions from their fellow workers. Ultimately the team members must sell the standardized process to employees not on the team. Sometimes this is not an easy job.

In libraries, one of the most successful approaches we have seen for recruiting a team is for the sponsor and team leader to send an invitation to potential team members (figure 3-5). This may seem like a trivial waste of time when the employees could just be assigned to the team, but experience shows that people like to feel they have some choice in the matter. In fact, some people excuse themselves for personal reasons from time to time—with no negative consequences.

When the team meets for the first time, it is important for its members to establish how they will work together. Even though they may work together every day on normal library activities, they rarely work together the way they will work in the process mastering team. In this team, they all have an equal say; setting team norms is the beginning of this new working relationship. If the team is going to understand completely and standardize the process, everyone must participate and contribute, so it is imperative that they agree upon rules for the team at the first meeting.

Vigo County Public Library Charter #2
REGISTER FOR/UPDATE A LIBRARY CARD
May 25, 2005

Team Members: **TERRI BROUGH-CONVENER, AMY INSERRA, JEFF TRINKLE, BARBARA WEAVER**

Purpose	▪ Create a process master (flowchart, screens, key tasks, and measures) that documents the process to "REGISTER FOR/UPDATE A LIBRARY CARD." Test the process master and revise it until any staff member can use it to complete the process.
Product/ Expected Result	▪ Written document including charter, flowchart, screens, key tasks, and measures, which has been thoroughly tested with staff members not on the team.
Authority	▪ May add up to two additional staff members who are not members of the Continuous Improvement workshop to the team.
	▪ Seek advice from staff members or others outside the library, as needed.
	▪ Spend up to three hours per week working on the process master.
	▪ Travel to or consult with other libraries in Indiana or Illinois to view or discuss borrower registration policies and procedures.
	▪ Request from systems staff special reports from SIRSI regarding borrower registration statistics and status.
	▪ Request from SIRSI special reports regarding library borrower registration statistics and status. Note: These are costly reports and authorization for report must originate from library director.
	▪ Travel to the site of the meeting.
	▪ Spend up to $200 on supplies for the meetings.
Limitations (Don't fail to)	▪ Consult with all library departments in creating or testing the process master.
	▪ Consult with Libby Walker and the Systems staff in creating or testing the process master.
	▪ Submit spending proposals to library director prior to authorization to spend allotted funds.
	▪ Note special report costs from SIRSI. Must obtain prior authorization from library director for special reports.
	▪ Obtain proper purchase orders from Business Office.
	▪ Inform library director if the team is getting behind schedule or needs assistance.
	▪ Submit all changes in borrower registration policy to be adopted by the Vigo County Public Library Board of Trustees (Note policy, not procedures, needs to be reviewed and adopted by Library Board)
Reporting	▪ Report weekly on progress using the Breakthrough listserv
	▪ Written report presented at the Breakthrough session on July 26

Figure 3-4 *Charter, Vigo County Public Library.*

Team norms are the rules of operation that define how a group has decided to manage its work (see Laughlin et al. 2003, 66–68). They make explicit what behaviors are expected and appropriate in the team; they shift responsibility for the operation of the team from the leader to the team as a whole; and they allow and require any member of the team to remind others of failure to meet the expectations and behaviors listed in the norms.

It is a simple matter and takes but a few minutes to establish norms at the first meeting. The team leader asks what rules everyone on the team wants to follow and lists the responses on a flipchart as the team members share their expectations, pet peeves, and desires. Typical areas of agreement include meeting times and arrangements (about food, temperature, cell phones, etc.), preparation for and follow-up after meetings, how individuals will treat each other, and how the group will make decisions.

The list of norms should either remain on the large chart paper and be posted at all meetings or be transferred to the minutes so that everyone has a copy readily available at every meeting. This makes it easy for everyone to be reminded about what they agreed to do. See figure 3-6 for an example.

Step 3.3
Flowchart the process.

At this point, the team gets down to business and comes to grips with "the process." For the first time, the team members must understand and agree on the name and scope of the process. Theoretically this was done earlier by the sponsor and the team leader, but it is common for the people involved with the process daily to see the boundaries of the process very differently. Once the flowcharting begins and the breadth and complexity of the process become clearer, it may be necessary to scale back the size or adjust the boundaries of the process being mastered.

Figure 3-5 Invitation to join team, Lawrenceburg Public Library.

"REGISTER FOR A NEW ADULT LIBRARY CARD" PROCESS MASTERING TEAM

Group Norms

- Be on Time
- Come Prepared
- Don't Take Things Personally
- Be Open to New Ideas
- Only One Person Speaks at a Time
- Consensus Rules
- Start and End on Time
- Everyone Brings Appropriate Tools
- What Happens in the Meetings Stays in the Meetings
- Treat Each Other with Respect

Figure 3-6 Group norms for "Register for a new adult library card" process mastering team, Vigo County Public Library.

Step 3.3.1 Agree on the tasks in the process.

Using flipchart paper, sticky notes, and markers, create a top-down flowchart (see Laughlin et al. 2003, 54–58). Begin by writing the name of the process on the top of a flipchart page. If it has not already been agreed upon, discuss and agree on the first and last tasks of the process. Write those tasks on sticky notes and stick them on either side of the flipchart page. As a team, brainstorm the intervening tasks. Each sticky note should represent a single task and start with an action verb. See the examples in figure 3-7, where the first task is "Verify ID" and the last is "Give patron VCPL borrower's card."

Try to think of the large general tasks in the process and write sticky notes for those tasks first. Stick those across the top of the flipchart in the order the work flows—from left to right.

Continue listing tasks that come to mind in the process. The scribe writes the task on a sticky note and attempts to place the sticky note in logical order on the flipchart. Soon it becomes obvious why the team is using sticky notes that can be readily moved, reworked, or discarded: some sticky notes are out of order, some overlooked tasks are discovered and added, some people call a task one thing and others call it something else, and the team finds itself in a bit of a mess.

The mess is normal—and it is real. It is not just that team members cannot describe their process. It may be that the process is done in several different ways by different people, in different locations, and at different times of day. The process may include tasks that no one can explain and that do not seem to be related to anything. The discussion that takes place while the team is attempting to organize the tasks is the first step in creating a shared understanding of the process.

Step 3.3.2 Put the tasks in order.

The team continues adding all the unique tasks in the process and placing them in the order they occur. True to the top-down flowchart approach, at the end of the exercise the team will have a series of high-level general tasks that flow from

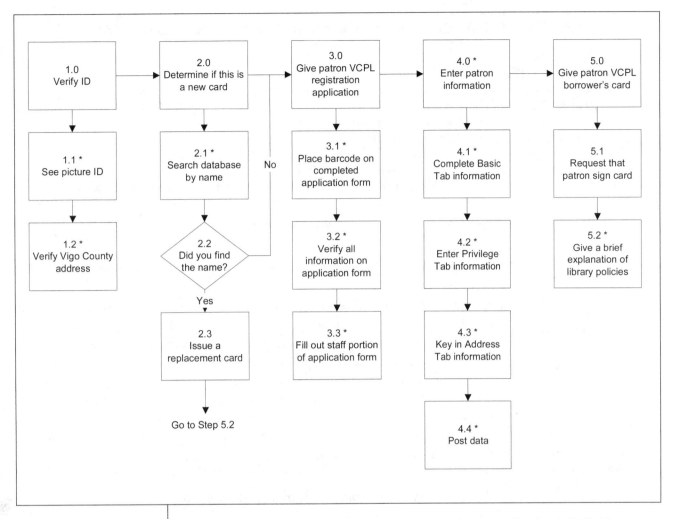

Figure 3-7 Flowchart of "Register for a new adult library card" process, Vigo County Public Library.

left to right across the top of the flipchart. In a vertical line, below each general task, will be an ordered flow of the actual tasks that take place under each general task. In figure 3-7, for example, the actual tasks under "Give patron VCPL registration application" are "Place barcode on completed application form," "Verify all information on application form," and "Fill out staff portion of application form."

About this time in the flowcharting experience, the question usually comes up, just how detailed do we need to be? The answer is, it depends. To some extent it depends on the reason for doing the process master. Will it be used for training? Is the process very complicated? Is the process not working? Is the team inventing a new process? In any case, remember that what the team is describing in the flowchart are the *tasks*

"REGISTER FOR A NEW ADULT LIBRARY CARD" PROCESS MASTERING TEAM

Parking Lot

- Revise Patron Registration form.
- Use other departments to help with discharging when Lending Desk gets busy.
- Develop a bookmark that explains how to access a patron account through our OPAC.
- Try using palm/handheld devise to register patrons and for other circulation functions.
- Examine the current use of guardianship documents.
- Change graphics on current bookmarks.
- Include all pertinent VCPL borrower information in our welcome brochure.
- Make sure all adult parents realize that they are responsible for items on their children's library cards too.

Figure 3-8 Example "parking lot," Vigo County Public Library.

We have found that what ended up in the Parking Lot will become a very important part of a revised process to place materials on reserve. . . . the simple act of creating an informal flowchart and sitting down to discuss this procedure has resulted in identifying the vagaries and gaps in the process. Clarifying existing tasks and creating new ones from the Parking Lot should result in . . . cutting down the process time from request to reserve.

—Kenyon Wells, Melvil Dewey Library and Media Center, Jefferson Community College

in the process and not particularly *how they do them*. Process mastering deals with the *what* first and the *how* to do the tasks later.

When the question of detail comes up, the scribe should put an asterisk on the sticky note to indicate that there is more to this task. The team will revisit these tasks later.

The team is temporarily finished with the flowchart when everyone is reasonably satisfied that all the tasks are listed and placed in the order they naturally occur in the process.

What if everyone cannot agree on the tasks or the order? Two suggestions: go back to the process and watch different employees do the process, or ask others who do the process what their opinion is on the question. One way or another, the tasks and order must be agreed upon. Many times it doesn't matter which way is chosen. What is most important is for everyone to do the process the same way.

Step 3.3.3   *Put improvement ideas in a "parking lot."*

As the flowchart develops, someone often comes up with a brilliant idea about how the process can be improved. The team should resist taking action on this, unless it is so amazingly obvious that it can be implemented with no effort and the benefits are great. Otherwise, the idea should be captured in a "parking lot" (figure 3-8) of ideas for future consideration (see Laughlin et al. 2003, 94–96).

Step 3.4
Identify key tasks with screens of customer and supplier needs.

It is not unusual for people doing a process inside a library to forget that the ultimate purpose of the process is to satisfy a customer. The customer may be external, a user of the library or a stakeholder, or internal, another staff member or unit of the library. It is useful and sometimes enlightening for the process mastering team actually to think about who those customers are and what they need from the process. The mastering team can do this in a structured way using external and internal customer screens, which help identify tasks that are key to meeting customer needs (figure 3-9).[4]

Every process also has suppliers, on which it depends for supplies delivered at the right time to support the process. Through a supplier screen, the process mastering team identifies what the process needs from its suppliers.

Step 3.4.1 Identify tasks important for meeting needs of external customers.

An external customer is anyone outside the walls of the organization, a "patron" or "end user," anyone who gets a product, service, or knowledge as a result of the process under study.

The actual mechanics of screening work best if the leader draws a large blank screen on a flipchart, asks each question in the same order, and then as the team answers the questions simply writes the comments in the screen at the proper location.

Completing screens for external and internal customers and suppliers yields two important benefits. It inspires rich discussion about who the customers are and what they need from the process and who the suppliers are and what the process needs from them. And the team benefits from discerning which process tasks are and are not important for satisfying customers and which tasks depend on suppliers' performance. This gives the team insight into which tasks are critical to perform well, and it sometimes points out tasks that are missing from the flowchart.

The first step in completing an external customer screen is to list the external customers who get something from this process. Sometimes this is easy. For some processes, however, it is not easy, and team members may have to stretch to think about who benefits from the process. Sometimes there are many external customers, and the team may choose to list only the most important ones or list categories of customers such as children, retirees, or job seekers. In figure 3-9, for example, an external customer screen for the "Register for a New Adult Library Card" process, the card applicant is the only external customer. If this had been a more general process of registering for a library card, external customers such as youth and out-of-county individuals may have been listed as well.

Next the team considers what external customers need or want from the process and writes several of the most important needs on the "External Customer Needs" section of the screen. In figure 3-9, the

EXTERNAL CUSTOMER SCREEN

Vigo County Public Library
Process: Register for a New Adult Library Card

External Customers: Card applicants

How strongly does the task affect the external customer need?
5 = Critical to meeting the external customer need
2 = Some impact on meeting the external customer need
0 = No impact on meeting the external customer need

Process Tasks Most Important to Meeting the Needs	Receive a VCPL borrower's card	Check out library materials	Reserve meeting rooms	Place holds on materials	TOTAL (add across each row)
Verify ID (1.0)	5	1	1	1	8
Give patron VCPL registration application (3.0)	5	4	3	1	13
Enter patron information (4.0)	5	5	2	2	14
Give patron VCPL borrower's card (5.0)	5	5	5	5	20
Give brief explanation of library policies (5.2)	0	5	5	5	15

Figure 3-9 External customer screen, Vigo County Public Library.

team thought that what these customers wanted most was to receive a VCPL borrower's card, check out library materials, reserve meeting rooms, and place holds on materials.

After the customers' needs are identified, the team asks which tasks in the process are most important for satisfying these needs? The team chooses tasks from the flowchart created in step 3.3 to add to the "Process Tasks " section of the screen. In figure 3-9, for example, the team selected five tasks from the flowchart that they believed were important for meeting external customer needs: "Verify ID" (task 1.0), "Give patron VCPL registration application" (3.0), "Enter patron information" (4.0), "Give patron VCPL borrower's card" (5.0), and "Give brief explanation of library policies" (5.2).

The team may find several tasks that are important for meeting the customer's individual need. They can list several. The team may also find that, for some of the needs, the important task has already been listed. They don't have to list that task again. Occasionally a team may not be able to identify any tasks in the process that meet an identified customer need. This might offer clues about why the process is troublesome or might reveal that a task was left off the flowchart.

To test and quantify the importance of the team's choice of process tasks, the team's next job is to evaluate each task against each need, using the following rating scale:

5 = Task is critical for meeting this customer need.

2 = Task is somewhat important for meeting this customer need.

0 = Task has no impact on meeting this customer need.

For example, in figure 3-9 the team asked, from a customer's perspective, how important is verifying a person's ID for getting a library card? They decided that it was very important, so they put a 5 in the box at the intersection of the task and the need. You will notice elsewhere in the screen that, although we suggest using only the 5, 2, and 0 values to ensure dispersion, this library chose to use any number between 0 and 5.

Repeating the question for the same task for the customer's second need, the team evaluated and recorded the findings. For example, in figure 3-9, the team asked how important verifying a person's ID is for checking out library materials and then rated the impact of this task to the external customer a 1. The team continued this evaluation until all the tasks had been evaluated for all the customer needs. They then added the numbers for each task and entered them on the "Total" line.

Step 3.4.2 *Identify tasks important for meeting needs of internal customers.*

In this step, the process mastering team repeats the screening procedure, this time focusing on internal customers' needs and the tasks in the process that meet those needs. By definition, processes have outputs that go to customers. Many times those customers are fellow employees who take the output from one process and further transform the output in a new process. If the first process can give the next process (i.e., the next-in-line internal customers) just what they need just when they need it, the whole system begins to improve.

The procedure for completing an internal customer screen (see figure 3-10) is exactly the same as that for an external customer screen. For the "Register for a New Adult Library Card" process, the team identified four internal customer groups and five important tasks. Using the screen, they agreed that tasks 1.1 ("See picture ID") and 1.2 ("Verify Vigo County address") were tied as most important to satisfying these internal customers.

INTERNAL CUSTOMER SCREEN

Vigo County Public Library

Process: Register for a New Adult Library Card

Internal Customers:

All check-out staff (branches, Young People's, Main Lending)
Staff updating completed application forms
Reference staff
Community Service/Literacy Learning Center/Administration

How strongly does the task affect the internal customer need?
5 = Critical to meeting the internal customer need
2 = Some impact on meeting the internal customer need
0 = No impact on meeting the internal customer need

	Internal Customer Needs				
Process Tasks Most Important to Meeting the Needs	Patron record with current information	Informed patrons	Completed applications	Valid VCPL borrower's card	**TOTAL (add across each row)**
See picture ID (1.1)	5	0	4	5	**14**
Verify Vigo County address (1.2)	5	0	4	5	**14**
Verify all information on application form (3.2)	4	0	5	0	**9**
Enter patron information (4.0)	5	0	0	5	**10**
Give a brief explanation of library policies (5.2)	1	5	3	0	**9**

Figure 3-10 Internal customer screen, Vigo County Public Library.

Step 3.4.3 Identify tasks that depend on supplier inputs.

Every process needs inputs, and these inputs come from suppliers (which can be external or internal, as you realized in completing the internal customer screen). In this step, the team reviews what the process needs from suppliers and which tasks are affected by these needs.

List the suppliers to the process. Remember that suppliers may provide materials, services, or information. There may be few or many suppliers. If there is a long list of suppliers, just list the most important ones or put the suppliers into general categories. The supplier screen in figure 3-11 shows examples of suppliers.

On the right section of the supplier screen, list the most important supplies that your process needs from these suppliers. On the left, list the tasks in which your process uses the supplies. Because in this case the team is evaluating the impact of the supply on the process, the direction of questioning is reversed. In this instance the team asks how important a supply is to this task in the process and places a 0, 2, or 5 at the intersections of the two items being evaluated. In figure 3-11, for example, the team asked, how important is the blank library card to "Give patron VCPL borrower's card"? and rated the importance of the supply a 5.

Continue doing this evaluation until all the supplies have been evaluated for all the tasks listed. Then total the numbers to see which supplies are most important to the process. Note that the total is at the bottom instead of to the right as it was in the customer screens.

Now we realize we need the process master for communicating with [our consortium], which does our cataloging.

—Pat Davis, Newburgh (NY) Public Library

Step 3.4.4 Identify tasks that meet library needs.

Using the team's accumulated understanding and information from the three screens and its own experience, return to the flowchart for a final look from the staff perspective.

SUPPLIER SCREEN

Vigo County Public Library
Process: Register for a New Adult Library Card

Suppliers:

> Business Office
> Mail & Supply
> VCPL Patrons
> SIRSI Library Automated System
> Systems Department

How critical is the input to completion of the process task?

5 = Critical to completing the step

2 = Some impact on completing the step

0 = No impact on completing the step

What Process Tasks Use Inputs from Suppliers?	What Inputs Does the Process Need Most from Suppliers?				
	Blank library cards	Applications	Barcodes	Automated library system	Computers
Give patron VCPL borrower's card (5.0)	5	3	5	3	3
Give patron VCPL registration application (3.0)	0	5	5	0	0
Post data (4.4)	0	4	5	5	5
Enter patron information (4.0)	0	2	0	5	5
TOTAL	5	12	15	13	13

Figure 3-11 Supplier screen, Vigo County Public Library.

Step 3.5.1 *Number each task.*

In the figures in this chapter, tasks have been neatly numbered. In real life, the team may still be adding tasks or shifting the task order throughout the flowcharting and screening. Now that the team has reviewed the tasks in the flowchart from several different viewpoints and perhaps added missing tasks, it is safe to finalize the numbering of the flowchart tasks. Label the high-level general tasks 1.0, 2.0, 3.0, . . . across the top of the page and the tasks under each general task 1.1, 1.2, 1.3, 1.4, . . . See, for example, the task numbering in the flowchart in figure 3-7.

- Does this task need further explanation for a novice to do it?
- Are there frequent mistakes or rework associated with this task?
- Is there a safety hazard associated with doing this task?
- Is there a measurement taken at this task?

The tasks identified through the screens and staff assessment are key tasks that require further investigation. They have been determined to be important to a successful, predictable process outcome.[5]

Step 3.5
Document details of key tasks on key tasks worksheet.

By this point in developing a process master, the team has a good sense of all the tasks involved, as described in the flowchart. They have thought through the needs of internal and external customers and developed an understanding of the process tasks that are most important from the external and internal customer screens. With the supplier screen they have identified the tasks that are dependent on high-quality supplies. They also know from their own experience which tasks in the process are complicated and which ones result in problems and time wasted redoing work.

Step 3.5.2   Record information about key tasks on the key tasks worksheet.

The team now considers whether each task needs further explanation, so that any staff member can complete it in a manner that satisfies customers and meets library needs. The team discusses which tasks need detailed explanation. Then, using a worksheet similar to the one shown in figure 3-12, they transfer the numbers and names of the key tasks from the flowchart that need a detailed explanation.

For each key task, team members develop a concise explanation about how the task is performed. Their agreed-upon standard way of doing the task should be written in the "Best-Known Way" column in the worksheet. This is often when the fun begins. It becomes clear at this point that everyone does not do the task the same way. But this is what is required if the process is to be standardized. Sometimes reaching agreement is easier said than done. There can be heated debate. The team may choose actually to go to the process site and try several methods of doing the task before deciding the best-known way.

There are two things to keep in mind at this juncture, when the team is trying to identify the "best-known way." The team should not get too hung up on the word "best." It is more important to standardize by choosing one way than to worry whether it is the best way. It is also normal for people to feel creatively threatened at this point. They think that standardizing everything will be boring and lead to loss of creativity. The exact reverse is true. Once the tasks and process are standardized, creativity can be turned loose trying to figure out how to do it better. Harnessing creativity to improve processes is discussed in chapter 5.

The team may want to use pictures, drawings, screenshots, other visual references, or references to standard operating procedures (if they are available) instead of simply writing text to describe the "best-known way." Some organizations use short video clips when they save their process masters on their internal websites.

Step 3.5.3   Add tricks of the trade.

The next step is to ask, are there any tricks of the trade in dealing with this task? Invariably a few team members share some of their wisdom about little-known methods that get the job done easier or faster. This is an opportunity for the more experienced members of the team to share their expertise.

Step 3.5.4   Describe consequences if the key task is done wrong.

The last step in discussing the key task is to ask, what are the consequences if this task is done wrong? Generally the answers to this question are straightforward, such as, "The customers don't get what they asked for," but sometimes at this late stage of the process master development there is an "a-ha" that is truly valuable. Team members may realize that they missed a task in the process, or that they have an opportunity to forestall a problem by adding a task or otherwise ensuring that it cannot be done wrong.

The team completes a key task description for each task on the flowchart that is starred, as shown in the flowchart (figure 3-7) and the key tasks worksheet (figure 3-12).

KEY TASKS WORKSHEET

Process: Register for a New Adult Library Card   **Date:** July 11, 2005

Team name: Vigo County Public Library Charter #2   **Date for recheck:**

Key Task #	Key Task Name	Best-Known Way	Tricks of the Trade	Consequences of Doing This Task Wrong
1.1	See picture ID	1. Patron must provide a picture ID such as driver's license, state ID, student ID, employee badge, Sam's Club, etc).		If patron does not provide a picture ID, we cannot issue a card.
1.2	Verify Vigo County address	1. Patron must provide proof of address if current address is not listed on picture ID. 2. In addition to driver's license or state ID, patron may provide one of the following current documents: • Rent receipt • Lease agreement • Utility bill • Preprinted checks • Pay stub • Vehicle registration • Voter's registration	1. Ask patron for picture ID with current address. 2. If address on ID is not current, list other options—start with rent receipt and proceed down the list. 3. Ask patron not to put away ID and proof of address until after application is completed and verified.	If patron does not provide proof of address, we cannot issue a card.
2.1	Search database by name	1. Search by last name only. 2. Scan the search results, looking for patron's first name. 3. Scan the search results, looking for suffix (Jr, Sr, II, III, etc).	If you don't find the last name: 1. Search in Alt ID field in User Display. Enter social security number without dashes or spaces. 2. If patron has had a card and previous searches have failed to produce a record, ask if card was under a different name. Search by alternate name (maiden, adopted, hyphenated, nickname, etc.).	• Get wrong person. • Overlook patron's record. • Will not bring up patron's record.
3.1	Place barcode on completed application and form	1. Place one barcode on application. 2. Place other barcode on card. 3. Check to see that the numbers match.	Remove both barcodes at the same time to ensure they match.	Barcodes on application and card may not match.

Figure 3-12 Key tasks worksheet, Vigo County Public Library.

Key Task #	Key Task Name	Best-Known Way	Tricks of the Trade	Consequences of Doing This Task Wrong
3.2	Verify all information on application form	1. Verify name and address printed on application match the patron's ID. 2. Make sure patron signed the form. 3. Make sure everything is legible. 4. Verify e-mail address, if necessary.	If patron's handwriting is not legible, print above so it can be read.	• Information will not be entered correctly. • May have to put a stop on the patron's card and gather correct information, causing inconvenience to patron.
3.3	Fill out staff portion of application form	1. Initial application. 2. Date application. 3. Indicate whether the application is New or Renewal. 4. Check the type of ID used for verification. 5. If type of ID used is not listed on form, write it in under "Other."		• If there is a question about the application and there are no staff initials, it is impossible to tell who processed it. As a consequence, the card may need to be stopped so the patron can be questioned. • If staff portion is not completed, it will be impossible to tell if ID was verified and/or what type of ID was presented. • If it is not indicated whether the application is New or a renewal, it adds work for updating staff, since they must then investigate so as not to skew the statistics. • If the type of ID presented is not indicated, it may be possible the card was issued to someone who is not a resident of Vigo County and does not actually qualify.
4.0	Enter patron information	1. Open User Information and Maintenance wizard. 2. Select New User wizard. 3. Scan barcode. 4. Choose Adult profile from dropdown menu. 5. Click OK.		• Barcode may be incorrect. • Profile may be wrong. • If you don't click OK at the end, you cannot proceed to the next task.

Key Task #	Key Task Name	Best-Known Way	Tricks of the Trade	Consequences of Doing This Task Wrong
4.1	Complete Basic Tab information	1. Enter patron's name in the name field (Last, First Middle). 2. Enter social security number in the Alt ID field (no dashes). 3. Enter patron's birth date in the Group ID field (mm/dd/yyyy). 4. Proceed to Privilege Tab. (Do not click OK or Enter.)	When registering a patron, all information should be entered in capital letters.	• If we can't search by name, we won't be able to access the record. • Data mailers will print the name incorrectly. • If social security number is not entered correctly, the system will not issue an alert if the number is already in the system. As a result, the patron will have a duplicate record. • If staff member hits OK or Enter, it will close the record. It will be necessary then to re-enter the record to enter the rest of the patron's information.
4.2	Enter Privilege Tab information	1. Change PIN number to last 4 digits of patron's phone number. 2. Enter override code to save change.		If PIN number is not entered, patron will not be able to access the account through online catalog.
4.3	Key in Address Tab information	1. Enter patron's address as given on the application in the street field. 2. Enter City and State on City/State line. (Do not enter comma after city.) 3. Enter zip code on Zip line. 4. Enter telephone number.		We can't send notices to the patron.
4.4	Post data	Enter patron data.		Patron information is not added.
5.2	Give a brief explanation of library policies	Use the script.		• Patrons won't feel welcome. • Patrons forget key information.

Handling Exceptions

When the automated system fails, ask the patron to fill out the necessary patron registration form. Save the form and the card until the system comes up, so you can determine if this is a new card or a renewal. Once you have determined patron status, enter all the data into the system. Mail the card to the patron. When the system is down and you take the completed patron registration form, allow new registrants to check out two items. Do this by keeping a written log of the patron ID barcode along with the subsequent item barcodes, so you can enter these into the system when it comes up.

Figure 3-12 Key tasks worksheet, Vigo County Public Library (cont.).

Step 3.5.5 Give directions for handling exceptions.

Even with everyone's best effort, sometimes there are exceptions. Things happen. Suppliers ship things in a little different manner. Computers go down. It is the job of the process mastering team to consider such occurrences. The team thinks about when in the past the staff had to deviate from the standard way of doing the process. They list these exceptions and describe how to do the process when the exception occurs.

If the exception happened once or twice and the consequences were minimal, it is not necessary to worry about it. But if the exception has happened numerous times and can be expected to happen in the future, it is a good idea to capture the exception and how to deal with it at the bottom of the key tasks worksheet. Notice, for instance, that the Vigo County Public Library (figure 3-12) recorded what to do when the automated system fails.

Step 3.6
List tools, equipment, supplies, and information required.

This process master step is as simple as its name implies. A good place to start is with the inputs provided to the process by suppliers from the supplier screen. Beyond that, list incidental supplies that are consumed in the process—tape, labels, ink, and the like. List the equipment required to do the process. Something as trivial as scissors is important if it isn't where it is supposed to be and time is wasted looking for it. Do not list things like a table or desk or lights or computer if they are always there. In figure 3-13, for example, we see that, for the "Register for a New Adult Library Card" process, the team needs blank library cards, barcodes, applications, computers, and the SIRSI system.

For some processes, information and other intangibles are important supplies. If these are not available at the right time and in a usable format, the process cannot proceed. Don't overlook these supplies. In figure 3-14, for example, the process "Send acknowledgment letters" occurred infrequently at the SUNY–New Paltz Library. Every time, the process was troublesome. As the team worked on the process, they discovered that most of the inputs were information from a variety of suppliers. They realized that they could not complete the process accurately and on time without high-quality information from them. Their list of tools, equipment, and supplies included member cards, copies of check/

**"REGISTER FOR A NEW ADULT LIBRARY CARD"
PROCESS MASTERING TEAM**

Tools, Equipment, and Supplies
- Blank library cards
- Barcodes
- Applications
- Computers
- SIRSI system

Figure 3-13 Example tools/equipment/supplies list, Vigo County Public Library.

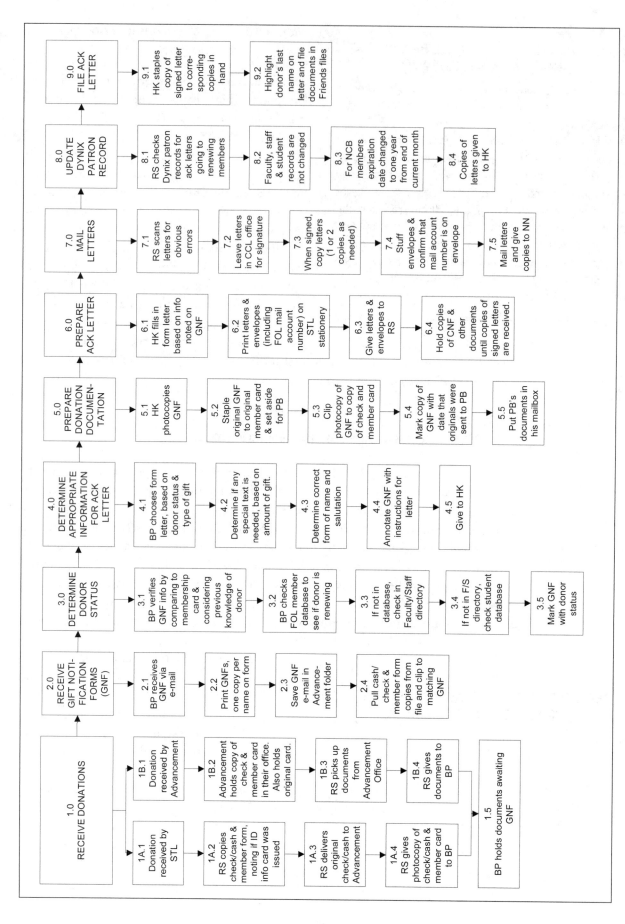

Figure 3-14 Flowchart for "Send acknowledgement letters" process, SUNY–New Paltz Sojourner Truth Library.

cash, gift notification forms (GNF), member database, faculty/staff directory, student database, form letters, Sojourner Truth Library stationery and envelopes, Friends of the Library mail account numbers, Dynix patron records, staplers, and highlighters.

As in this SUNY–New Paltz Library example, some processes in every library are done infrequently, and thus having a process master is important to remind everyone how to do it. Likewise, it is important to have a complete list of the tools, equipment, supplies, and information required to do the process before it is begun. If any one of them is missing, the process will be interrupted and time lost. Think about your coffee break room, for instance. Do you frequently find that the coffee, filters, creamer, or some other supply has been used up? At the Chicago Public Library, we saw a simple solution. Right above the coffee station in the staff development department, a piece of paper was taped to the wall, with a pencil dangling on a string. Everything was right there for anyone noticing that supplies were low to write it on the list. Everyone in the department benefited from this simple solution.

Step 3.7
Test the process master.

Now that the process master is complete, put it together in draft form and try it out in the library. For those on the process mastering team, there may be a few surprises as they ask others to test the process master. Usually the supervisor or team leader introduces employees to the process master, answers their questions, and asks them to try it. The team leader encourages employees to observe and note how clear the process master is and if anything is wrong or missing.

A second way to test the process master is to ask someone who does not normally do the process to try to do it, using the process master. Some teams ask the sponsor of the team to give it a try. This is an excellent way to give feedback to the sponsor and to get recognition for the team.

The testing is critically important. Team members must approach it with enthusiasm and with high expectations that the rest of the employees will try the process master with an open mind. If there is a culture of learning and acceptance of change, there will be little hesitation on the part of the employees. If this is not the present culture, then this step is an opportunity for leadership and trust building.

During the test period in which several testers have had several opportunities to try the process master, the team gathers all the comments and suggestions.

Step 3.8
Review the trial and modify the process master.

After the testing, the team reconvenes and discusses the comments, suggestions, and experiences result-

---

LAWRENCEBURG UPDATES PROCESS MASTERS

After two years of steady effort, the Lawrenceburg Public Library had created a process master for every circulation process; process masters were kept in a portable file at the circulation desks in the main library and at the branch. New circulation staff members referred to the process masters regularly, and some part-time staff reported that they used them when faced with tasks they performed infrequently, but most full-time staff didn't need them often. Recently, when the library installed a new integrated library system, the circulation staff realized their process masters no longer reflected the way they did many routine processes. The newest member of the staff worked for several weeks to modify the process masters by documenting the new tasks, then asked other staff to test the new process masters. Other staff members were very complimentary of her work and report that they are still turning to the process masters for those processes that they use less frequently and can't quite remember.

ing from the test. If required, they make changes to the tasks in the process master, then put it into final form.

This is also a good time to discuss any ongoing responsibilities, such as who will be gathering and plotting the measures for the process and who will be the official "process owner" in charge of keeping track of the process master after the team has completed it. How and where will the data be displayed? How will exceptions to the process master be handled and tracked? How will the team deal with deviations from the process master that may be observed?

Step 3.9
Sign on and take responsibility.

The final step in creating the process master is for the team to accept the process master formally and celebrate its completion. The team might have a public ceremony to sign the cover page of the document. If the document is electronic, the team might be acknowledged there.

The cover of the process master includes the following items:

- Name of the process

- Date and any other identifying information needed to keep track

- Statement or a declaration such as the following: "This process master has identified and documented the best-known way to carry out this process. By signing below, we agree to follow the process master whenever possible. We understand that exceptional situations may force a temporary change in the process. When this happens, we will act in the best interest of our customers. We will turn in an exception report of temporary changes for possible updating of the process master. We will also be constantly on the alert for ways to improve the process."

- Signature/acknowledgement of the sponsor, team leader, and all team members

Now that the process master is finished, what does the team and the library do with it? To a great extent this depends on how it is recorded. If the document is on the library's intranet, then it is available at all computer terminals. Managing updates and access to the file on the computer is discussed in chapter 6.

If the process master is in print, there should be a copy at the location where the process is performed. Some organizations put key operational parts of the process master such as the flowchart and key tasks worksheets under glass near the work area. Some laminate the operational sheets for durability when use is frequent. Some put the process master in a notebook or filing box and store it near the work area. What is important is that the document be used. It should not be shelved, never to see the light of day again.

Step 3.10
Deploy the process.

At this point, all in the organization need to know that this is the way they are going to do this process from now on—until they find a better way. In a small organization this is a simple matter, because many people have been involved in doing the process master. But in larger organizations with several shifts or locations, this may need to be communicated formally. Don't forget to inform any suppliers or customers who may be affected by the newly standardized process.

Step 3.11
Monitor use of the process master.

It is now up to the team leader and team to use the process master and constantly encourage everyone to follow it. Even with a process master, there is a tendency for processes to become sloppy. Everyone within the process must remain vigilant in monitoring to ensure that the methodology does not wander. Often it is logical to have the process team leader become the process owner, to make sure that everyone continues to follow the process master and that any future changes are agreed upon and incorporated. Read more about the process owner's ongoing responsibilities in chapter 6.

CONCLUSION

Standardizing a process by creating a process master is the first step in process improvement. A sponsor initiates the process mastering by creating a charter, which specifies the team leader and team members, the product, the authorities and limitations, and the reporting requirements for the team.

The team begins by setting team norms. Through discussion, they reach consensus on the "best-known way" to do a process. They document the tasks of the process in a flowchart and identify the key tasks in the process through screens of external and internal customer needs and needs from suppliers. To the flowchart tasks identified through the screens, they add any tasks important to the library, decide which tasks are key to the process, and document them in a key tasks worksheet along with tricks of the trade and supplies. They invite colleagues to test the draft process master, make modifications as necessary, and then publish and agree to follow the completed process master. They choose a process owner to oversee ongoing use and updates.

In the next chapter, we discuss choosing a measure that will give the team information about the performance of the process.

NOTES

1. Some of the material in this chapter has been adapted from Wilson and Harsin (1998), with permission from the publisher.
2. The library may choose to use some different titles for the various sections of the charter, but the effect should be the same. Note that after several process mastering charters have been written, a pattern will be established and the charters will become somewhat standardized.
3. A good book for organizing and running teams that are working on continuous improvement is Scholtes et al. (1996). Tools for working in teams are also included in Laughlin et al. (2003).
4. The team may use a spreadsheet for the screen, in which they can enter formulas to calculate totals, or a word-processed table, as shown here.
5. Some organizations treat every task as a key task and detail them all on the key tasks worksheet. Note that some of the process tasks in the customer screens may end up with high totals but can still be ignored as key tasks because they are simple and don't require elaboration.

Chapter 4 | **Measure Process Performance**

Every process must have at least one measure to track how it is performing over time. Why measure processes? After all, libraries have always gathered and reported data to local boards and state agencies. They have carefully measured inputs—number of staff, size of collection, square footage of facilities, or size of budget. They have kept track of outputs such as registration, circulation, gate count, and program attendance. More recently, some have attempted to measure outcomes—customer awareness, satisfaction, increases in knowledge or skill, or improvements in condition.

Although these numbers are necessary for reporting and give a general picture of the productivity of the library, they are the accumulation of dozens of processes over hundreds of hours. Take, for example, a single circulation. Before the item is checked out, it has to be selected, ordered, received, cataloged, labeled, and shelved correctly. To be able to retrieve it and check it out, the customer has to be entered correctly into the customer database. Think of all the processes involved. For the transaction to be smooth, all of those processes have to be working smoothly and efficiently. But how would you know if they were?

Something dramatically different is needed to measure these daily processes. The team wants to know quickly if the process is working well, so that it can make changes if it isn't. Team members want to be sure that, when they do make an intervention, they are not tampering with the process in a way that negatively affects its function.

In chapter 3 your team created a process master. The team probably generated a "parking lot" full of good ideas for improving the process and are anxious to begin. Now they need measurements to see how their process is doing and to decide if they need to work on improving the process. After they launch improvements, they need data to understand if the process is getting better, staying the same, or getting worse.

In this chapter we help the team decide upon a measure for its own process and give the members a tool for recording and beginning to study their data to decide if the process needs improvement. For many this is a paradigm shift, so do not be surprised if you have to put this book down for a little while or talk to some others involved in quality improvement before it "sinks in." It is not rocket science, but it is a radically new way of looking at numbers.

> *In the absence of an adequate and appropriate measurement system, it's virtually impossible to improve the performance of a manufacturing or business process, increase customer satisfaction or ensure the quality of product or service.*
> —Ronald D. Snee (2006, 72)

Step 4.1
Decide upon a measure for the process.

Every standardized process must have at least one measurement indicating how it is doing on an ongoing basis. This is a new kind of data, different from the traditional measures that libraries have collected and reported for years. It is not likely that the library is already collecting the data needed to measure processes.

This is a place where many teams get bogged down, for a variety of reasons: It is difficult to find a good measure; some people don't really want to know how poorly the process works and fear retribution; some assume that it will involve a lot of extra work when they already feel overwhelmed; and some are skeptical of the value and validity of this kind of data.

But gather data they must, if they are to improve their process. They have to understand how the process is doing now. They have to know if their changes are improvements or not. The approaches in this chapter help address all of these points of resistance.

Finding Things to Measure

Figure 4-1 is a picture of places to look for measurement opportunities. You will recognize that it is the general system with suppliers and customers, to which has been added a decision-making box labeled "Process management and improvement." The figure may help your team investigate all the avenues of possible measurements—supplier performance, input characteristics, process changes, process and employee measures, output, customer feedback, and even benchmark comparisons with other organizations.

Perhaps the most important measures are those related to customer (external and internal) needs or desires. You must satisfy the customer. Review the external and internal customer screens. Who are the customers? Do the customers' needs suggest something to measure? Are measures possible at the key tasks you have already identified as related to customers' needs?

Conversely, figure out what outcomes your customer doesn't want, like wasted time, frustration, misinformation, feeling foolish and hassled. Learn how to measure what the customer wants and doesn't want. And remember: there are internal as well as external customers.

If you are working on improving the process, it is often most efficient to work upstream—within the process and toward the supplier side on the diagram. This is where you can make small changes and reap big improvements.

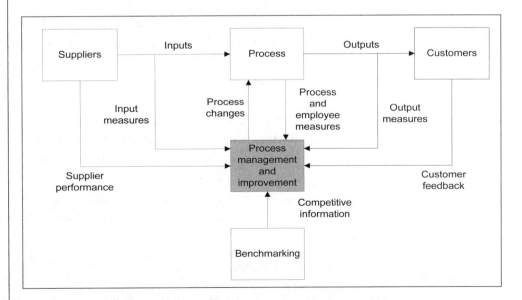

Figure 4-1 Flowchart of measurement ideas. Reprinted from Hoerl and Snee (2002, 75), with permission of the authors.

If you just want to see how good your process is (or is not), check out how other organizations measure your particular process. Don't limit your thinking to other libraries. Other organizations also order things; receive, move, and inventory things; pay bills; store things; answer questions; orient new employees; clean and maintain facilities; schedule meetings; collect fines; select and ship things. Compare your library to the best in the library business—or in some other business.

Don't worry about measuring the wrong things. If you find out that the measure you choose is not important, stop gathering data and choose something else to measure. In the meantime, you have learned something. This is another reason to gather data as rapidly as you can. You learn faster. Also, you will find that you get better at choosing measures with experience.

General Criteria of Practical Measures

As the team begins to consider what to measure, several questions help frame its decision:

Is the measure developed by consensus of the team? Because the data will be collected by those involved in the process, agreeing what to collect, when, and how is key to successful measuring.

Is the measure practical to implement? Choose measures that don't take much time or expense to collect. Some measures may be collected, for example, by the library's computer systems and require no staff intervention at all. Others may be collected on a sampling basis—during one hour a day or a typical week, or by collecting one hundred transactions, for example.

Is the measure easy to understand? The tools in this chapter help you create visuals for studying and presenting data. As the team develops measures, it can ensure that they are understandable by sharing them with other staff and listening carefully to their questions and suggestions.

Is the measure specific? The evaluation "It seems better" does not meet our minimum standards as a measure. Qualitative observation is sometimes acceptable, but only if it is controlled and intentional. To study the process and any changes you make, you need quantifiable data that you can plot on a chart.

Does the measure generate data fast? You need twenty points of data to be able to say anything credible, so if you wait for twenty years of annual circulation totals, you'll be missing many opportunities for improvement. For processes that are done daily, think how you could get a point of data daily. Measures taken weekly or monthly are fine if that is as often as the data are available. The sooner the team can see the current performance of its process, the sooner it can intervene and make improvements.

Are we sure the measure won't cause harm? This might sound silly in libraries, where in most cases collecting data is not dangerous. But it's worth thinking about.

Types of Measures

Process measures are quite different from the measures most libraries have in place. Appendix B lists library process measures that may serve as a starting point in understanding this new kind of measure and as a resource when the process team chooses measures. Process measures frequently fall into one of five categories: *time* (elapsed time, wait time, cycle time); *cost* (or cost savings); *quality* (often measured by error rate); *customer satisfaction* (complaints, suggestions, compliments); and *quantity* (productivity, throughput, capacity). Specific examples of measures chosen by library process teams that fit each of these categories are described below.

Example A: Elapsed Time

Patrons and staff at the Lawrenceburg Public Library were complaining about how long it took for new books to reach the shelves. The technical services staff decided to study the process of preparing books for circulation. The team flowcharted the process and made many discoveries along the way. They identified seven major tasks. Because the library is small, each of these tasks was essentially completed by one employee. As they discussed the tasks, the individuals learned—many for the first time—what happened in the tasks before and after their own.

The team already knew that the measure of their process must be the time elapsed from beginning to end of the process, that is, from the time the book was removed from the packing box until it was ready to shelve. But how could they keep track of the elapsed time without adding to their own workload and further slowing their process? The team decided to add a slip of paper inside each book. The employee who unpacked the box recorded the initial date on the slip. As each task was completed, the employee recorded the date before passing the book on to the next station. When the process was complete for that book, the slip was forwarded to a department assistant, who computed the number of days from the beginning to the end of the process. At the end of each week she entered the data from each completed slip into a spreadsheet to compute an average for all the items completed that week and recorded that number, along with any notes about exceptional situations like library closings, staff illness, or automation anomalies.[1] Figure 4-2 shows the data for the first twelve weeks of 2003 and of 2004.

Example B: Cycle Time

A continuous improvement team at Pace University Library sensed a problem in turnaround time in getting METRO ILL books to the Graduate Center (which is not a METRO delivery site) from other Pace libraries. They collected data and found that turnaround time averaged eighteen days. They decided to try changing the drop-off site for the Graduate Center items from the Law School in White Plains to Mortola in Pleasantville. They collected data between April and July 2004 and found that the average turnaround time dropped to nine days. On the basis of this data, they decided to make the change permanent.

Example C: Cost Savings

A Vigo County Public Library team created a process master for "Select gift books." They decided to count the number of gift books received each week at each library location and in five general categories—paperback "rack" books, fiction, nonfiction, large print, and reference; they added audiovisual formats after they realized they were also receiving gifts in other formats. They tracked the number of gifts acquired by the library over a

Task Definitions:

A: Unpack Date to Holding Shelves
B: Holding Shelves to Cataloged
C: Cataloged to Item Entry
D: Item Entry to Physically Processed
E: Physically Processed to Item Data Checked
F: Director Looks at First Copies of Title Only

Week	Average Days to Complete Each Task						Total Days
	A	B	C	D	E	F	
2003							
January 6-10	10.625	7.050	1.725	1.675	2.350		23.430
January 13-17	9.370	7.209	2.193	3.822	6.048		28.642
January 27-31	6.952	4.337	7.648	1.903	2.089		22.292
February 3-7	4.517	5.337	4.717	4.544	3.427	1.301	23.843
February 10-14	9.815	9.358	3.092	4.427	4.355	0.066	31.113
February 17-21	7.026	6.493	2.600	9.386	4.773		30.278
February 24-28	5.790	5.320	1.630	5.440	9.736	1.933	29.849
March 3-7	5.299	3.060	2.821	6.313	9.194	0.000	26.687
March 10-14	6.117	10.013	0.870	2.195	5.650	0.909	25.754
March 17-21	3.217	5.116	0.091	2.630	3.116	1.000	15.054
March 24-28	7.072	12.800	1.681	4.147	1.928	1.411	29.039
March 29-April 4	6.945	5.200	2.300	3.612	1.728	1.000	20.785
2004							
January 5-9	3.875	1.396	1.938	1.167	1.417	0.935	10.728
January 12-16	9.871	4.452	0.484	1.129	2.419		18.335
January 19-23	8.909	2.455	0.545	1.636	4.682		18.227
January 26-30	3.167	0.100	1.067	1.022	4.178	0.526	10.060
February 2-6	1.083	8.000	1.250	1.125	2.625	0.000	14.083
February 9-13	4.333	1.867	1.405	1.976	6.133	0.235	16.188
February 16-20	1.556	0.630	8.407	0.667	1.148	1.000	13.408
February 23-27	3.773	0.848	4.424	1.015	1.439		11.499
March 1-5	1.552	0.241	3.310	1.000	3.690	0.111	9.904
March 8-12	1.962	0.132	1.396	3.755	5.566	0.000	12.811
March 15-19	5.158	0.079	3.960	2.178	4.931	0.700	17.006
March 29-April 2	0.638	0.447	8.447	1.404	2.085	1.000	14.021

Figure 4-2 Data collected on time required to catalog books, Lawrenceburg Public Library.

three-week period, the number given to the Friends for the book sale, and the number discarded. Of the 3,602 total books donated, the library discarded twelve, gave 2,451 to the Friends, and added 1,139 to the collection (figure 4-3). Using price estimates, they computed the value of the gift books acquired by the library and arrived at an estimate of cost savings of $3,075 per week, or an annual estimated savings in excess of $150,000. As a result of this study, the library realized it could rely on gifts to meet some of its customer demand for paperbacks (especially romances), so it shifted some of its book budget away from paperbacks and into other areas.

Week	Library Location	Discards	Friends	Rack	Fiction	Non-fiction	Large Print	Reference	AV
8/15-19/2005	Lending	4	147	75	37	10	0	0	47
	North Branch	0	7	71	2	1	5	0	0
	South Branch	0	39	244	4	11	2	0	1
	East Branch	0	31	0	4	3	1	0	2
	West Branch	0	0	1	7	2	0	0	0
	Reference	0	163	0	2	0	0	0	1
	Tech Services	0	43	115	31	18	0	0	11
	Young Peoples	0	0	0	2	3	0	0	0
8/22-26/2005	Lending	4	166	16	5	11	0	0	4
	North Branch	0	95	37	0	2	0	0	0
	South Branch	4	182	17	5	5	0	0	0
	East Branch	0	58	2	9	4	1	0	0
	West Branch	0	0	1	1	0	0	0	0
	Reference	0	618	0	9	8	0	0	0
	Tech Services	0	25	6	13	20	1	1	10
	Young Peoples	0	58	82	13	5	0	0	0
8/29-9/2/2005	Lending	0	98	23	4	8	0	0	0
	North Branch	0	20	4	1	0	0	0	0
	South Branch	0	117	4	2	0	0	0	0
	East Branch	0	16	2	1	0	0	0	0
	West Branch	0	0	7	0	0	0	0	0
	Reference	0	511	0	80	0	0	0	0
	Tech Services	0	57	13	42	23	0	0	4
	Young Peoples	0	0	0	3	1	0	0	0
	Total	12	2451	720	274	134	10	1	80
	Total Discarded	12							
	Total to Friends		2451						
	Total to Collection								1139
	Grand Total Books								3602
	Total AV								80

Figure 4-3 Data collected on gift books received, Vigo County Public Library.

Example D: Errors

The Cazenovia College Library had abundant data about its first-year seminar bibliographic instruction program. The library staff taught a twenty-minute session for nineteen first-year seminar classes in mid-September 2003. After the class, the library sent a "General Library Knowledge Survey" to the seminar instructors and recommended that they allow their students a few weeks to become more familiar with the library before administering the survey. The instructors then administered the survey during a class period or allowed the students to treat it as a take-home exercise. The students returned their completed surveys to the instructor, who forwarded them as a unit to the reference librarian, who scored them. To pass, a student had to answer at least twelve of the twenty questions correctly. Figure 4-4 shows the percentage of students who passed for each of the seventeen instructors who submitted completed surveys in 2003/4. The library also had detailed data about the pass/fail ratio for each question.

Example E: Satisfaction

The Mishawaka-Penn-Harris Public Library was interested in improving its technology training for staff, but first it had to understand what kinds of help its customers needed with technology. They asked the staff at every public service desk to record the types of customer technology requests they received (figure 4-5). After a week, they were already beginning to see where to focus their staff training efforts.

Example F: Quantity

The new director of the Benton County Public Library felt that handling interlibrary loan was taking an increasingly large share of her time. She decided to study data already available about the number of packages the library handled each month. Figure 4-6 includes two years' worth of data.

Example G: Quantity (Throughput)

The staff at New York University's Bobst Library studied customer complaints and noticed that many of them involved hours of operation, especially on Saturdays. They used a

Year	Faculty	Percent Pass	Faculty	Percent Pass
2004	1	100.0%	10	100.0%
	2	76.9%	11	7.7%
	3	55.6%	12	60.0%
	4	100.0%	13	6.7%
	5	50.0%	14	25.0%
	6	88.9%	15	36.4%
	7	100.0%	16	28.6%
	8	77.8%	17	100.0%
	9	35.7%		

Figure 4-4. Data collected on bibliographic instruction posttest pass rate, Cazenovia College.

Figure 4-5 Data collected on customer requests for assistance with technology, Mishawaka–Penn–Harris Public Library.

Task	Main Requests June 12	13	14	15	16	17	T	Bittersweet Requests June 12	13	14	15	16	17	T	Harris Requests June 12	13	14	15	16	17	T	Total
Print in Color	3	0	0	0	4	12	19							0							0	19
Enlarge Pictures for Printing			3				3							0							0	3
Inspire							0							0							0	0
Referred							0							0		1					1	1
Show How to Use							0							0		1					1	1
Other Database Assistance							0	1		2				3							0	3
Help with the Unemployment Website	4	0		3		2	9							0							0	9
Internet Assistance in General	17	18	25	19	7	19	105	4		3		4	3	14	1	1		1			3	122
Setting Up an Email Account	1	0	0	0	0	0	1			1				1				1			1	3
Scanning Assistance		6			1		7							0		4				1	5	12
Microsoft Word	16	7		13		11	47	1						1							0	48
Microsoft Excel							0							0							0	0
Microsoft PowerPoint							0							0							0	0
Microsoft Access							0							0							0	0
Microsoft Publisher							0							0				1			1	1
CD-Burning Assistance			15	13	2	4	34							0						1	1	35
Computer Troubleshooting	13	26	18	14	6	12	89						2	2	1	1	1		1		4	95
(Computer Freezing, etc.)							0							0							0	0
Miscellaneous	4	1		5		2	12	1						1	2	2	2		1		7	20

Month	Total Packages	Month	Total Packages
Jan-01	26	Jan-02	54
Feb-01	16	Feb-02	51
Mar-01	42	Mar-02	105
Apr-01	34	Apr-02	98
May-01	17	May-02	59
Jun-01	51	Jun-02	157
Jul-01	51	Jul-02	77
Aug-01	66	Aug-02	68
Sep-01	117	Sep-02	89
Oct-01	52	Oct-02	90
Nov-01	34	Nov-02	56
Dec-01	86	Dec-02	75

Figure 4-6 Data collected on packages handled, Benton County Public Library. Notice that the data will be reoriented from columns to rows in order to create a run chart.

run chart to plot the number of circulations per hour (figure 4-7). When their chart confirmed the students' obvious preference for later hours, they changed their Saturday hours. There was no grumbling among the staff, since they could see from the chart that the decision made sense.

Considerations about Data and Measures

As you think more deeply about possible measures, there are additional nuances to consider. Some measures are *measurements*. They can generally be distinguished by the fact that you can select the degree of precision. For instance, if you are measuring time, you can decide to measure days, hours, minutes, or seconds; if you are measuring temperature, you can choose the number of decimal points to include. Other examples of measurements are time from receipt to shelf, waiting time, time between accidents, value of inventory, cost of damaged items, customer satisfaction, worker's compensation cost, turnover rate, minutes of system downtime, preventive maintenance hours, overtime, and distance.

In the previous examples, Examples A (elapsed time), B (cycle time), C (cost savings), and E (satisfaction) are measurements, since all of them can be expressed with more or fewer decimal points.

Some measures are *counts*. Examples are the number of data entry errors, wrong shipments, damaged items, overdue notices, customers served, Web hits, employee absences, instruction sessions, suggestions implemented, adults who learned to read, or donors.

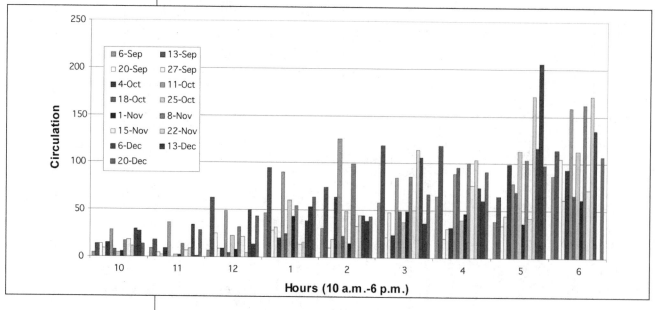

Figure 4-7 Data collected on circulation by hour, New York University.

Counts can be further defined as *counts of events,* such as number of requests, complaints, customer visits, cataloging errors, or *counts of items.* When you are counting items, you are generally counting items with an attribute, such as number of shipments that are incorrect, number of suggestions implemented, number of items that are damaged, or number of data entries that have errors.

In several of the examples above, the teams chose to use counts: D (errors), F (quantity), and G (quantity/throughput).

When you study this short list of examples or look at the list of library measures in appendix B, it soon becomes apparent that much depends on how you phrase a measure. How do you count suggestions from customers? Do you count the number of suggestions per week, or do you count the number of customers who give suggestions per week? This is the kind of question team members must discuss when choosing what and how to take a measure of their process.

An additional consideration when dealing with counts is something called the "area of opportunity"—"the region within which the counts occur. It has to do with what is being counted, how it is being counted, and what possible restrictions there might be on the count" (Wheeler 2003, 199). The question is, how variable is the reservoir of data from which the counts might come?

Consider this case. A process mastering team working on the book-shelving process has decided to track the number of misshelved books. They plan to do this by reading shelves daily. Figure 4-8 shows the number of shelves read and the number of misshelved items found in the first ten days of reading shelves. The question is, will the team get a correct sense of the quality of the shelving process if they plot the number of misshelved books discovered daily? The answer is no, because their area of opportunity varies too much from day to day. Reading as few as two and as many as ten shelves per day is too large a disparity. So how do you decide what is too much variation in the area of opportunity?

According to one rule of thumb, "When the areas of opportunity vary more than ±20 percent from the average size of the areas of opportunity, you should convert counts into rates before plotting them on a process behavior chart" (Wheeler 2003, 210). Using the data in figure 4-8, here is how the team analyzed their situation. They found the average number of shelves read per day by adding the shelves and dividing by ten days—55 divided by 10 resulted in an average of 5.5 shelves per day. Twenty percent of 5.5 is 1.1 ($5.5 \times 0.20 = 1.1$). They added 1.1 to 5.5 and got 6.6; they subtracted 1.1 from 5.5 and got 4.4. Thus, to be within the 20 percent range, the number of shelves read would have to vary only between 4.4 and 6.6 per day. From figure 4-8 it was apparent that several days were higher or lower than the allowable 20 percent deviation. They therefore turned the resulting counts of misshelved books into a ratio, or percentage. (The ratios for the first two days are $6/4 = 1.5$ and $1/5 = 0.2$.) Because the area of opportunity was larger than 20 percent, the team plotted the ratios rather than simply plotting the counts.

Most times with careful forethought the measure chosen will be correct for the situation. If, after several data points have been gathered, the team determines that the measure must be tweaked, it isn't the end of the world. The team will have learned something.

Step 4.2
Set timeline and assign responsibility for taking the measure.

To be sure that the data are valid and to reduce the chance of introducing outside variation into measures (whether measurements or counts), it is critical that the team specify

- exactly what will be measured
- when (time of day, week, or month) it will be measured
- how it will be measured (count, instrument, calculation, etc.)
- who will do the measuring

Use figure 4-9 or something similar to document your decisions for future reference, and make it part of the original process master document.

Step 4.3
Gather data about the process.

Using the measure the team has chosen and the procedure they have agreed upon, begin to gather data.

Day	Number of Shelves	Misshelved Items
1	4	6
2	5	1
3	8	2
4	6	7
5	10	2
6	2	4
7	7	2
8	4	1
9	5	0
10	4	3
TOTAL	55	28

Figure 4-8 Data collected on misshelved items.

Step 4.4
Create a run chart.

Look again at the data in figure 4-2. What can you say about the process? You can see that some tasks account for more of the time than others. You can see considerable variation from one week to the next. You notice that there are no data for task F during about half of the weeks. Is the process stable? Is it meeting customer expectations? Answers to these questions are a little hard to find among so much data when it is presented in table format.

Creating a run chart helps the team see patterns in the data and find the average of all points. A run chart is also the first step in applying statistical tools to create a process behavior chart (see chapter 5), the best way to understand whether variation in the data is just normal variation or indicates that the process has changed.

Process: _____

Measure: _____

Measurement or Count? _____

If a count, is it a count of items or a count of events? _____

What is the count's Area of Opportunity? Describe examples and assumptions.

_____

When (time of day, date, etc.): _____

How to measure: _____

Who is responsible: _____

Date	Time	Who	Measure

...adding more rows as needed...

Figure 4-9 Measure description and record template.

Step 4.4.1 Record basic information about the process.

If you are creating the run chart by hand, you can use a chart similar to that in figure 4-10. Record the data on a worksheet similar to figure 4-11 to guide your calculations and document the results. Add the name of your process, the process owner, the date of your initial charting and calculations, and other relevant facts. It seems obvious, but you'd be surprised how quickly you forget and how confusing the chart becomes for others if you neglect to give them the context. In our example from the Lawrenceburg Public Library in figure 4-12, note that the process is "Catalog books," the unit of measure is days to completion, and the date calculated is April 15, 2003.

Step 4.4.2 Record your data.

The top row in figure 4-10 identifies the date or event. In the second row, write down the data points (Xs) as you gather the data. In figure 4-12, for example, the Lawrenceburg team decided to plot the total number of days (the right-hand column in figure 4-2). The numbers in the date row refer to week 1 (January 6), week 2 (January 13), week 3 (January 27), and so

BLAMING

When an organization uses measures in a significant way, it is not uncommon for people to think that individuals are to blame for the poor performance of a process. If this situation is not treated quickly and decisively, a culture of blame can arise. It is important to reiterate that more than 90 percent of the problems are a result of the process, not the people. It is incumbent on leadership to understand this point and to look at the people as the source of variation and poor process performance only as a last resort.

on. For the first week, the actual total on their chart was 23.430, but they decided to round the numbers to whole numbers, so they entered 23 right under week 1. Under week 2 they rounded 28.642 to 29 and added this to the chart, and then they continued to add the other ten numbers representing the weekly averages, rounded to whole numbers.

Step 4.4.3 Establish an appropriate y-axis range.

After you accumulate a reasonable number of data points (which depends on your improvement timeframe, frequency of taking a measure, etc.), choose an appropriate scale for the y-axis in the X/SAMPLE graph below the data. Because you will continue to gather data and add them to the chart and you'll be adding some statistical limits in chapter 5, leave substantial room at the top of your scale.

In the Lawrenceburg Public Library example (figure 4-12), the team glanced across the twelve points of data in their chart and saw that the lowest number was 15 and the highest 31. Thus, they set the y-axis range from 0 to 50.

Step 4.4.4 Plot the data points.

Plot each data point on the line directly below the number in the graph and connect the points with a line. See figure 4-12 for an example.

Step 4.4.5 Find the average.

After you have accumulated a reasonable number of data points, find the average of the data. Record the X_{AV} on the worksheet in figure 4-11 and add the average line to the graph on figure 4-10. (Don't worry about the bottom part of the worksheet, the process behavior chart section. We cover that in chapter 5.)

In our example, the Lawrenceburg group found the average of the Xs, (X_{AV}), by dividing the sum of all the values by the number of values (307 / 12 = 25.6).

Step 4.5
Display the run chart.

Display the run chart near where the process is done so that it is easy to plot new data points as they occur. This also allows staff members who work in the process to see the run chart and discuss it. They will be able to see if the process is stable and running smoothly or if it is changing. If they decide to initiate changes in the process, they will look forward to gathering data and plotting the next points to see if the change improved the results.

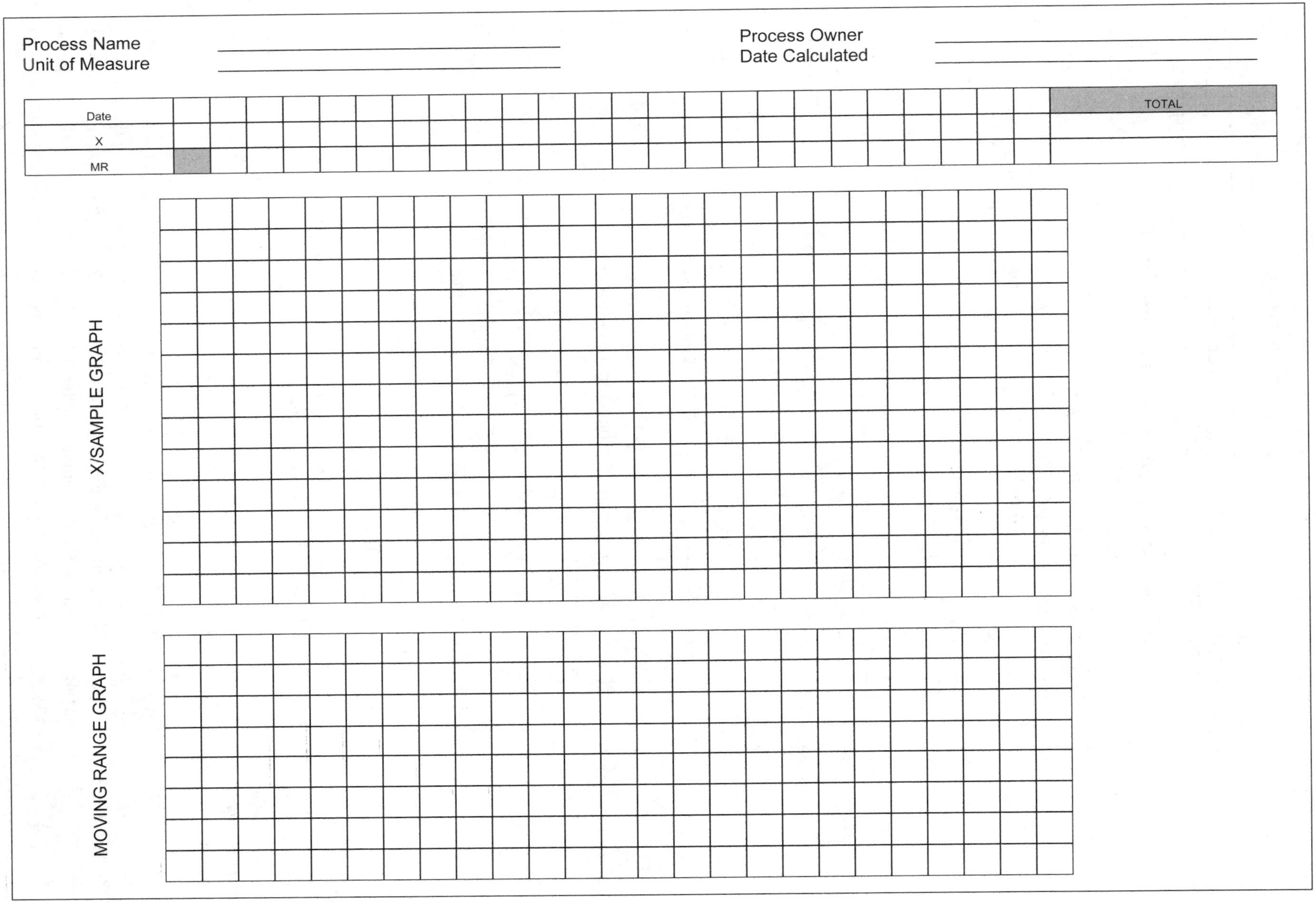

Figure 4-10 Run chart/process behavior chart template.

RUN CHART WORKSHEET

Process ____

Date Range ____

Process Owner ____

X_{AV} = Total all Xs ($X_1 + X_2 + \ldots$) and divide by the number of Xs.

X_{AV} = ______

Process Behavior Chart Worksheet

MR_{AV} = total all MRs ($MR_1 + MR_2 + \ldots$) and divide by the number of MRs (which will be one less than the number of Xs).

MR_{AV} = ______

$UPL_{MR} = MR_{AV} \times 3.267$ (get MR_{AV} from calculation above)

UPL_{MR} = ______ × 3.267

UPL_{MR} = ______

$S = MR_{AV} / 1.128$ (get MR_{AV} from calculation above)

S = ______ / 1.128

S = ______

$3S = S \times 3$ (get S from calculation above)

3S = ______ × 3

3S = ______

$UPL_X = X_{AV} + 3S$ (get X_{AV} and 3S from calculations above)

UPL_X = ______ + ______

UPL_X = ______

$LPL_X = X_{AV} - 3S$ (get X_{AV} and 3S from calculations above)

LPL_X = ______ − ______

LPL_X = ______

Figure 4-11 Run chart/process behavior chart worksheet template.

Doing things better equals improving the experience of customers, staff, and stakeholders in a way that is measurable, meaningful, and maintainable. Projects start with, and success is measured by, meeting customer wants and needs; data are collected and used to make good decisions.

—Shaunessy Everett (2006, 29)

Stop! Don't Change Anything Yet!

Avoid making any process-changing decisions until a significant number of data points have been gathered—ideally twenty or more.

CONCLUSION

For many libraries, measuring processes is new and challenging. Process measures frequently fall into one of five categories—time, cost, quality, customer satisfaction, and quantity.

Once a library process improvement team has completed a process master, it is ready to study the process and determine whether it needs improvement. The first step is to agree upon a measure or measures, considering whether a count or a measurement is more appropriate.

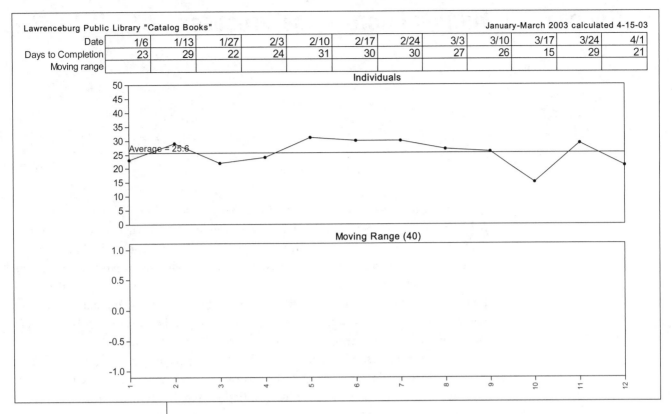

Lawrenceburg Public Library "Catalog Books"										January-March 2003 calculated 4-15-03		
Date	1/6	1/13	1/27	2/3	2/10	2/17	2/24	3/3	3/10	3/17	3/24	4/1
Days to Completion	23	29	22	24	31	30	30	27	26	15	29	21
Moving range												

Figure 4-12 Run chart for "Catalog books" process, Lawrenceburg Public Library.

Next, the team decides how, when, where, and who will collect the data and adds those decisions to the process master.

Third, they collect data and add each data point as it is collected to a run chart.

Finally, after they have collected a sufficient number of points of data, they create an average of the data points.

In chapter 5 we take you on the next stage of the journey of continuous improvement—using statistical process control methods to study your process, deciding whether it needs improvement, trying some changes, and studying them to see if they improve the process.

NOTE

1. The staff discussed whether to count weekends and holidays, when they were not working. They decided that they would, since those were days that customers were still waiting for books. They decided to include all books, regardless of source, rather than separating rental books, replacements, titles requiring original cataloging, and the like, since they could not devote the time to keeping records for all these subgroups.

| **Rapidly Improve the Process**

A t this point, you have standardized your process, settled upon a measure, and collected at least some data. Is the process producing the quality you want? In this chapter we discuss how to analyze your process and try some ideas for improving it.

After the completion of a process master, the people who do the work in the process are following the methods outlined in the process master. Everyone is sensitized and observant about how they are doing the tasks in the process. During the standardization, they may have already begun thinking about how they could do the process better, more easily, quicker. They were tempted to make some changes, but if they followed our advice they resisted the impulse and gathered the ideas for change on a "parking lot" of ideas.

In actuality, in almost every case, the process has already been improved simply by being standardized, since that has reduced variation. But it is human nature to want to make things better, and thus there is an urge to make more improvements. The power of this approach to improvement is that it enables employees to make changes rather than waiting for a supervisor or manager to tell them to make the changes. This is the time to let the process speak to you through the data being gathered.

As the points of data accumulate on the run chart, you observe several things. Not all points are the same; they vary from one measurement to the next. This is normal. Even with the best efforts to standardize, there is variation. Every now and then the variation may be much more than usual. Again, this is to be expected. The caution here is not to do anything as a result of an unusual variation. If you do, you may be doing something called "tampering"—and chances are you will make things worse instead of better.

Somewhere along the line, people begin to wonder: Is this too much variation? Is it normal to have this much variation? I wonder why this point is so much higher than the last? What should we do to make tomorrow's point go down? My eyeball tells me that the average of these data points is this; is this good or bad? Things still aren't very good; how can we make them better?

In the past, you may have ignored these comments or failed to reach agreement on what caused the variation or whether the average was reasonable. Some employees may have been concerned about the condition of the process; others may have explained why things took so long or why there were so many mistakes. They may even have blamed the problems on the supervisor, another department, or customers.

To answer these and similar questions, you need to do some statistical analysis. Before you close this book and say, "I didn't sign up for that," let us reassure you that hundreds of library employees have learned how to do the simple calculations necessary. You can too. It's not necessary (initially, at least) to understand complicated statistics to be able to use them to study your process. The results are visual and compelling. This is one of the

We knew we weren't supposed to change anything yet, but . . . when you see how stupid something you're doing is, you just want to change it.
—Judith Schwartz, Rachel Savarino Library, Trocaire College

most important things you can learn and apply to make correct decisions. In fact, once you learn it, you may ask yourself how much harm you have done previously before you learned how to do this.

A process behavior chart expands the value of the data in a run chart by applying some simple math.[1] Creating a process behavior chart takes just a few calculations. You can use it to analyze your process data in order to make the right decisions about the process.

At this point, it is important to remember one of the basic tenets about systems from chapter 1: more than 90 percent of the variation in the output of any process comes from the system, not from the people in the system. Things happen. Variation just occurs. It is not the result of people not trying their best. It is the result of variation in the process.

Before we proceed to learn about process behavior charts, we need to address the topic of appropriate number of data points. Statistically speaking, if you have twenty to twenty-five points of data and you do a process behavior chart, you can be 99.7 percent sure that the next point of data will be between the natural process limits calculated for your process. If you have fewer data points when you calculate your natural process limits, you will have less confidence in predicting the next point. This does not mean, however, that you shouldn't try with fewer points. You can get started. Just realize that your confidence in the data will not be as high as it would if you had more points. As a rule of thumb, remember that a few points of data thoughtfully chosen and consistently collected are much better than many points of data carelessly chosen and inconsistently collected.

Step 5.1
Create a process behavior chart.

Adding a few statistical controls to the run chart dramatically increases the information process teams can get from their process. Once a team has data, a process behavior chart is easy to create. A highly visual tool, it shows whether the process is in control (predictable) or not, how much variation is occurring, and whether the process is getting better, staying the same, or getting worse. Team members can also use it to spot cycles.

To construct a process behavior chart, begin with the run chart you created in step 4.4 in chapter 4. You have already completed the first five steps (refer to figures 4-10 and 4-12):

- Filled out the top of the process behavior chart with the name of your process, the process owner, the date of your charting, and other relevant facts.
- Recorded the data in the two top rows of the chart.
- Chose an appropriate scale for the y-axis on the X/Sample graph.
- Plotted the points on the top graph and connected the points with a line.
- Calculated the average and drew the line.

Leaving this graph for the moment, return to the third row in the data area, labeled "MR." Before we complete the top graph, we need to be sure that all our points are within normally expected variation. To do that, we complete the moving range graph at the bottom of the page.

Step 5.1.1 Calculate the moving ranges (MRs).

The *moving range* is the measure of variation from one point to another. Find the difference in value between the first X and second X in the second row and pencil it into the "MR" row below the second X in your run chart/process behavior chart (figure 4-10). Notice that the first box is empty, since two points are required to complete the first calculation. Do the same for the difference between points 2 and 3, 3 and 4, and so on. Note that it is the absolute difference between the numbers that is important. Record the number as a positive number, even if you get a negative number in your subtracting.

For our example in figure 5-1, the difference between the first X, 23, and the second, 29, is 6, which is recorded in the box under the 29. The difference between the second and third number is 7, and so on. Notice that the data and the top graph are exactly the same as in figure 4-12.

Step 5.1.2 Choose a range, plot, and connect the points.

As in step 4.4, choose an appropriate scale for your MR graph, plot the points at the bottom of the page, and connect the points with a line. For the Lawrenceburg example, figure 5-1 shows the MR range of 0 to 20, with the points plotted and connected by a line.

Step 5.1.3 Calculate the average MR (MR_{AV}) and draw a line across the MR graph at that value.

Add up all the MR values and divide the total by the number of MRs to get the average (MR_{AV}). Place the MR_{AV} value on the worksheet and draw a solid horizontal line at that

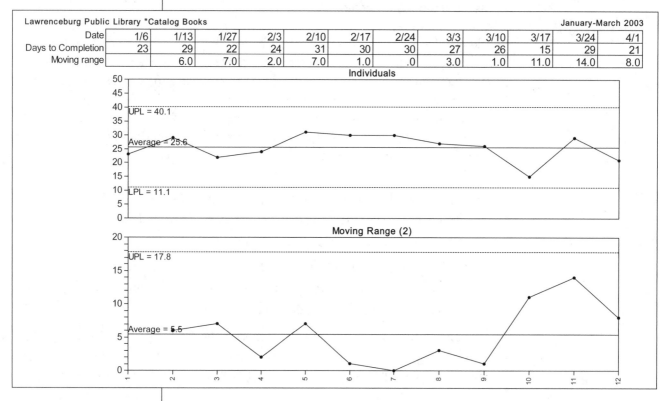

Figure 5-1 Process behavior chart for "Catalog books," Lawrenceburg Public Library.

value on the MR graph. In the example in figure 5-1, the team added the eleven values in the MR row for a total of 60 and divided by 11, for an MR_{AV} value of 5.45, which they rounded to 5.5. If they were using the run chart/process behavior chart in figure 4-10, they would have drawn a line at that value across the MR graph and recorded the value in the figure 4-11 worksheet.

Step 5.1.4 Calculate the upper process limit for the moving ranges (UPL_{MR}).

Calculate the upper process limit for the moving ranges (UPL_{MR}) with the following formula:

$$UPL_{MR} = MR_{AV} \times 3.267$$

The number 3.267 is a statistical constant derived from having a subgroup of two (R_1-R_2, R_2-R_3, . . .). For more information, see Wheeler (1992, 237). In the example in figure 5-1, the MR_{AV} is 5.5, so the team multiplied 5.5 by 3.267 and arrived at 17.8. Record the UPL_{MR} value on the worksheet and add the UPL_{MR} line as a dashed line across the MR graph, as in figure 5-1.

What does this line mean? The UPL_{MR} is the upper limit of expected variation, based on the average variation in the eleven points of data included. If the process is stable, the team can be almost certain that no points will appear above this line as long as the process doesn't change. If a point does fall above the line, they can assume that this point is anomalous, the result of a "special" cause. The next step explains how to check for this situation and adjust the calculations, if necessary.

Step 5.1.5 Check for special causes in Xs.

Are any individual MR points greater than the UPL_{MR}? If none is, assume that the variation is normal, that is, from "common" causes, and continue to the next step (calculate the standard deviation). In figure 5-1, none of the points is above the UPL_{MR}, so the team continued to the next step.

If a data point does fall above the UPL_{MR} line, it almost certainly represents a "special" cause. In order not to skew the calculations, recalculate a new MR_{AV} and then a new UPL_{MR} by ignoring the value of X that caused the MR point to be above the UPL_{MR} line.

Figure 5-2 illustrates a special cause point in an MR graph. In figure 5-3, the point has been excluded to avoid skewing the calculations; now all

---

TAMPERING AND VARIATION

Tampering as a result of measurements happens all the time in organizations. Managers see the data point go up or down from the last point and react by changing the process in an attempt to get the next data point to go the other direction. In most cases this process change only makes the process more variable and unpredictable.

There is variation in everything. You must expect the data points to vary from one measurement to the next. This normal variation has a name—*common cause* variation. Most of the time the causes are unknown. The variation could be caused by the humidity, the time of day, differences in the input, the mood of a worker, or dozens of other things. The key is that you dare not react to this unknown variation. If you do, you are tampering.

How can you know when you are dealing with common cause variation? When you have accumulated enough data to develop a process behavior chart, you can discern common cause variation—any data points between the upper and lower process limits (UPL and LPL). Any normally varying data points that fall between the process limit lines are common cause variation, and the process should not be changed as a result of the variation from point to point.

If, on the other hand, a point goes above or below the process limits or several points meet other statistical patterns, these points are referred to as having a *special cause*. In this instance, you should learn what caused this to happen. It might have been something unusual that caused the process to perform badly for a short time—a computer breakdown, a snow storm, or something similar. Or it might have been something that caused the process to perform beautifully, perhaps the result of a process improvement trial. If this is the case, you will want to change the process to make this a normal occurrence.

The goal is to reduce variation and to move the average in the desired direction.

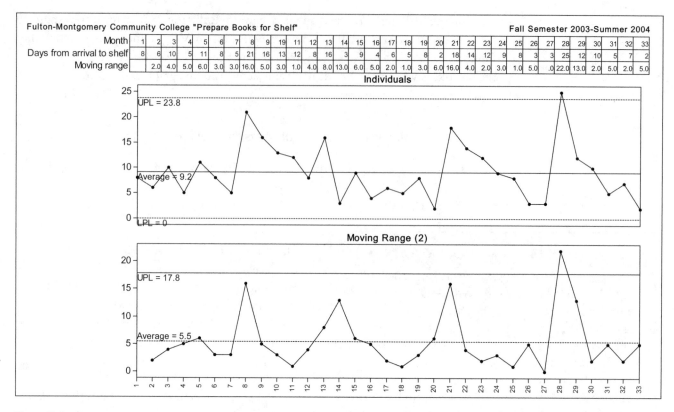

Figure 5-2 Process behavior chart for "Prepare books for shelf," Fulton-Montgomery Community College.

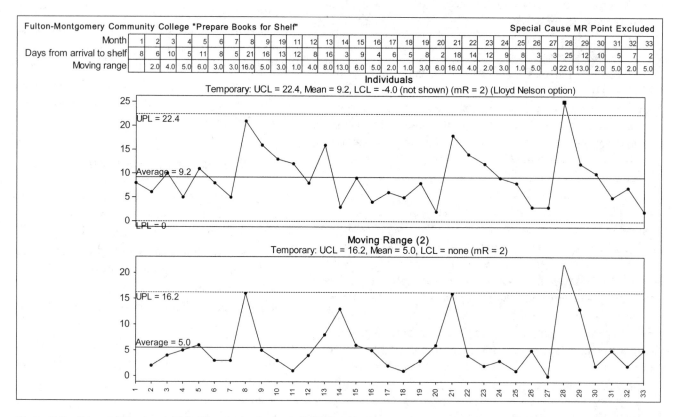

Figure 5-3 Process behavior chart for "Prepare books for shelf," Fulton-Montgomery Community College, adjusted to exclude special cause data point. Note the open point toward the right end of the moving range chart.

the MR points are below the UPL_{MR}. It is possible that you will have to do such correction routines more than once if one or more MRs exceed the newly calculated and plotted UPL_{MR}. If you are plotting points by hand, leave the Xs in the upper graph and plot them—just don't use them in the calculations.

Step 5.1.6   Calculate the standard deviation (S).

Calculate standard deviation (S) as follows:

$$S = MR_{AV} / 1.128$$

The number 1.128 is another statistical constant (see Wheeler 1992, 237). Record the value of S on the worksheet in figure 4-11.

In the Lawrenceburg example, team members divided 5.5 (their MR_{AV}) by 1.128 and got 4.84. They recorded that number on the worksheet and multiplied it by 3 (i.e., three standard deviations: $4.84 \times 3 = 14.5$), for use later in their calculations.

Step 5.1.7   Calculate the upper process limit for the Xs (UPL_X).

Calculate the upper process limit for the Xs (UPL_X) using the following formula:

$$UPL_X = X_{AV} + 3S$$

In the Lawrenceburg case, X_{AV} is 25.6 and 3S is 14.5, which total 40.1. This UPL_X value is recorded on the worksheet and as a horizontal dashed line on the X/SAMPLE graph (figure 5-1).

Step 5.1.8   Calculate the lower process limit for the Xs (LPL_X).

Calculate the lower process limit for the Xs (LPL_X) by applying this equation:

$$LPL_X = X_{AV} - 3S$$

In our example, subtracting the 3S value (14.5) from the X_{AV} value (25.6) produces an LPL_X of 11.1, which is recorded on the worksheet and drawn as a horizontal dashed line on the X/SAMPLE graph.

If the LPL_X is less than 0, ask yourself if such a value is possible in your process. If not, the LPL_X is 0 by default. In the figure 5-1 example, for instance, it is not possible to take fewer than zero days to prepare a book for circulation, so even if the team's LPL_X calculations had yielded a negative number, 0 would be the lowest possible limit.

Step 5.1.9   Make a visual check to be sure your graph makes sense.

Are the averages midway through the points on both graphs? Do they seem reasonable? Are the upper limits above and the lower limits below the data points on both graphs? If any points are above the limit in the lower graph, go back and check for special causes. If any points are outside the upper and lower limits in the upper graph, redo your calculations. Such points may be valid or not, as you see in step 5.2.

The real act of discovery consists not in finding new lands but in seeing with new eyes.
—Marcel Proust, from *In Search of Lost Time*

Step 5.2
Use the process behavior chart to learn about the process.

The process behavior chart is now complete and ready to be used to analyze what the process is doing.

Is the process predictable? When the Lawrenceburg Public Library team looked at their data in the process behavior chart (figure 5-1), they saw that the process was in control (predictable), showing variation from 15 to 31 days, with the average number of days required for preparing books for circulation equaling 25.6. The team could say with good assurance that the next and subsequent points would be between the upper and lower process limits unless they changed the process.

Is there a great deal of variation? In the moving range graph, the Lawrenceburg team observed a great deal of variation from one week to the next. They began to wonder if there were ways they could reduce it.

Is the average higher or lower than customers expect? The team was definitely not happy to discover that the average number of days from the beginning to the end of their process was 25.6. Even though they didn't have data, they knew they would have to add to that average the days necessary to select, order, and ship the materials, plus the time for the circulation supervisor and the director to inspect the books and to shelve the materials once they were delivered to the circulation desk.

Is the process getting better, getting worse, or staying about the same? For Lawrenceburg, the process behavior chart showed that the process was staying about the same.

Does the process go through cycles? Within the twelve weeks the team tracked data, they noticed that during some weeks many boxes of books arrived, while other weeks were very light. Could this have anything to do with ordering patterns? They learned from the acquisitions staff that the department batched orders until a certain dollar amount was reached. No one could remember the reason for this. Perhaps it related to shipping discounts or from the days when orders were printed and mailed.

Step 5.3
Improve the process using the Plan-Do-Study-Act cycle.

Now the team has standardized the process and has a clear picture of its average performance and of the variation within it. If they are fortunate, the process is performing well. Their customers are happy. The average for the process is just where they want it to be, and the process shows only minimal variation. If this is the case, they need only monitor the process by gathering some data regularly and adding it to the process behavior chart to be sure the average and variation remain in acceptable ranges.

But more likely, especially if this is the first time this process has been studied, the team discovers that there is room for improvement. Perhaps the average is too high or too low; perhaps the variation is too wide; perhaps both are unacceptable. No amount of wishing or browbeating of the employees will make the data get better. Unless there is a change in the process, the team can predict what the succeeding data will look like. So what should they do now?

Making changes in almost anything within an organization can be tedious. It does not have to be this way. In fact, it must not be this way if the library is to keep pace with the current challenges. The people who have mastered the process, who operate the process every day, and who have ideas about how to improve it must be empowered to change it for the better. It should not take long to see some results.

Ultimately, when an organization is transformed into a continuous improvement learning organization, everyone will be trained in continuous improvement tools and will know how to use and interpret process data. Quality will be embedded in the daily work of employees and the library. When that is happening, there is continuous innovation and challenging of processes to make them better.

To begin improving a process, use the charter to commission a process improvement team. The team may, but doesn't need to, consist of the same people who were on the process mastering team for this process. This new charter will be in the format discussed in chapter 3, but this time the purpose of the charter is to improve the process rather than standardize it.[2]

The team has been adding ideas to a "parking lot" throughout the process mastering and data gathering. Now is the time for them to unleash their collective creativity and try some improvements, with the data to guide them, of course. There is a straightforward structure for the team to use to do this. It is called *rapid cycle improvement.*

Rapid cycle improvement is based on asking three questions (Langley 1996, 4–10): (1) What are we trying to accomplish? (2) How will we know if a change is an improvement? (3) What change can we make that will result in improvement? Let's examine each question.

What Are We Trying to Accomplish?

The improvement begins when the sponsor and the team decide what they are trying to accomplish. Answering this question can take many forms. Sometimes the search for an answer to this seemingly simple question can take some digging. The answer is important, because upon it the team will experiment with improvements.

Fewer mistakes? Faster response? Lower cost per use? More predictable attendance for computer classes? More correct answers to reference questions? Lower turnover of employees? Fewer complaints about missing books? Higher attendance at programs? Faster turnaround of video and audio materials? Fewer copier breakdowns? Cleaner building? Better communications among staff? Fewer overdue notices? Improved community literacy? Less time spent on budgeting? Better space utilization? Less time spent fixing mistakes? More bills paid on time? Fewer damaged items? Fewer cataloging errors? Easier to use Web resources? Lower healthcare costs for employees?

One or more of the exercises already reviewed in this book may suggest an answer. The exercise of identifying key processes that support the library's key success factors (chapter 2) or process mastering (chapter 3) may clarify for the team what the library is trying to accomplish. Customers (external or internal) with their words and actions may articulate what needs to change. The process behavior chart data and the people doing the process may reveal room for improvement. Two examples illustrate how staff teams have answered this essential question:

Circulation staff at the Michigan City Public Library weren't sure exactly what the library was trying to accomplish. They asked their department head what the library was trying to do. The department head suggested that they make an appointment with the director and take a look at the strategic plan. In the plan, improving customer service was a key success factor. They realized that anything they could do to save time and communicate clearly and professionally with customers would be a contribution.

In a second example, faculty at a university in New York State were complaining about how long it took for newly acquired audiovisual materials to be available in the library. After the library team gathered data, they discovered that it took more than a semester for materials to be ready to circulate, so they knew what needed improving.

The Hazards of Setting Targets and Numerical Goals

Do libraries need to set numerical goals or targets to be successful? Generally, targets and goals are detrimental, according to W. Edwards Deming, who advised against setting arbitrary numerical goals.

Deming cited several reasons that targets and goals are not effective. First, targets frequently have no basis. He used the example of a manager setting a target of a 10 percent increase in sales for the next year. But why 10 percent, why not 12 percent? Until you can answer that kind of question, Deming concluded, any number will do.

Second, arbitrary numerical goals frequently backfire. Think about the example of Domino's Pizza, which used to guarantee delivery within 30 minutes. This target seemed fine to customers and gave the employees a goal. The 30-minute delivery guarantee no longer exists, however, because drivers drove unsafely and at high speeds in order to meet the goal. Failure to make the delivery on time was money out of their pockets. The company failed to consider traffic, the number of orders received and other internal variations, and the costs of lawsuits caused by the resulting accidents.

Third, goals engender fear of failure associated with not making the goal. This is an energy-wasting diversion from working to make the process or system better.

Finally, sometimes setting a target limits the improvement possible. It is human nature to work to achieve the goal and then stop rather than go on to exceed the target.

Do all targets or goals need to be arbitrary? Henry Neave suggested two other types of numbers that management can use (1990, 362–63): (1) Facts of life. If we don't make this profit figure, we will go out of business. (2) Planning, prediction, and budget. These can be used to compare alternative plans.

Although these two types of numbers seem pretty straightforward, they can be problematic and therefore must be considered carefully as well. Take, for instance, the "facts of life" target of needing to reduce costs by 10 percent to keep the company from going out of business. This might seem like the only choice in a desperate situation. In reality, though, the company may be able to earn more revenue and achieve the same thing.

Planning, prediction, and budget numbers are important. If they are used to decide among alternative approaches, such numbers can be useful. But their usefulness as planning numbers can be destroyed if they are turned into rigid targets without consideration for how to achieve them and for the consequences or fear engendered if they are not achieved. When the goals have consequences attached for individuals, people generally choose one of three responses: (1) distort the process or system in which they are working, for short-term or individual gain; (2) distort the numbers; or (3) improve the process or system in which they are working.

More often then we care to admit, people choose the first or second response to achieve the target. In libraries, for example, a circulation increase can be achieved when the branch manager checks out dozens of items herself. Conversely, if the target has been met, the staff may decide not to offer children's story hours. Or reference staff, afraid because business has been slow, may pad their reference log to reach last month's figures. Obviously it is more difficult and takes longer for the individual or team that chooses the third response—to improve the process or system.

To help the library avoid setting targets and goals, we offer a few ideas:

1. Resist strongly even discussing a goal or target until a sufficient number of data points are gathered—the more points the better.

2. Ask why a specific target or goal number is necessary.

3. Ask what decisions and actions might be taken to try to achieve a target number.

4. Ask what the consequences are for individuals and the organization if the target is not met.

5. Put the data into a process behavior chart before deciding if a numerical goal is warranted and, if it is, what it should be.

When the process behavior chart is constructed, the team will find out the average of the data points and the variation among them, and thus they will be able to make a strong prediction about what the data will look like in the future if the process is not changed. This is hearing the voice of the process or system.

If the voice of the process or system does not match the voice of the customer—what the customer wants—then the process or system must be changed. Sometimes the average of the data must go up, sometimes down. Sometimes the variation of the data must be reduced. In either case, if you have developed a process behavior chart the team is much better informed about the capability of the process or system and the gap between its results and the desires of the customer.

Even at this point, it is best to resist setting a specific target. Rather, suggest a goal to make the average move in the desired direction or to reduce the variation as much as possible.

Special Cases of Goal Setting

There are two special cases that must be discussed when considering measurements and goal setting—incentives and performance appraisals. When individuals are pitted against each other for rewards, the result is often cheating, falsification, and manipulation. At the very least, using measures in this way distorts the system and introduces variation. At the worst it can destroy the organization. Just don't do it!

How Will We Know if a Change Is an Improvement?

The answer to this second question can be found in the data, which obviously requires the team to have data about the process to begin their inquiry. The change, if any, in the data will show if a change in the process has resulted in an improvement. The simple statistics incorporated in the process behavior chart allow the team to be sure that the change is real and substantial and not just a short-term variation.

After team members decide to try a change (more about this in the third question, below), they continue to gather data on the process and add it to the process behavior chart. They extend the average line and process limits in the X/SAMPLE graph and MR graph so that they can easily see if the data begin to show improvement.

All improvement requires change, but all changes do not result in improvement. To be considered an improvement, the change must lead to higher value to someone—better quality, a lower price, or both.
—Gerald Langley
(Langley et al. 1996, 169)

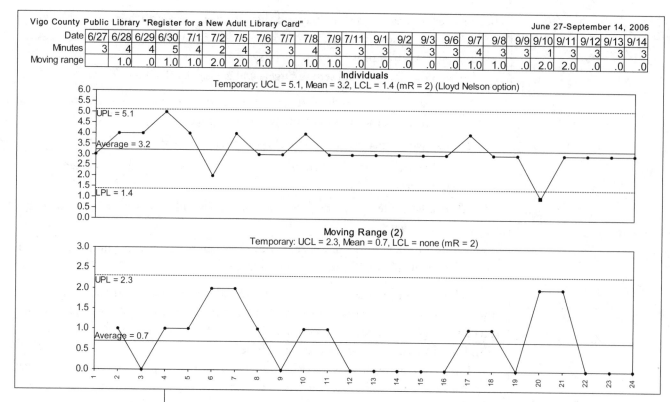

Vigo County Public Library "Register for a New Adult Library Card"																				June 27-September 14, 2006			
Date	6/27	6/28	6/29	6/30	7/1	7/2	7/5	7/6	7/7	7/8	7/9	7/11	9/1	9/2	9/3	9/6	9/7	9/8	9/9	9/10	9/11	9/12	9/13	9/14
Minutes	3	4	4	5	4	2	4	3	3	4	3	3	3	3	3	3	4	3	3	1	3	3	3	3
Moving range		1.0	.0	1.0	1.0	2.0	2.0	1.0	.0	1.0	1.0	.0	.0	.0	.0	.0	1.0	1.0	.0	2.0	2.0	.0	.0	.0

Individuals
Temporary: UCL = 5.1, Mean = 3.2, LCL = 1.4 (mR = 2) (Lloyd Nelson option)

Moving Range (2)
Temporary: UCL = 2.3, Mean = 0.7, LCL = none (mR = 2)

Figure 5-4   Process behavior chart for "Register for a new adult library card," Vigo County Public Library.

When a process behavior chart shows any of the following patterns, there is evidence that the process has changed (Wheeler 2003, 107–12). Until that time, the team cannot assume that the change has made a real difference to the process.

Pattern 1: Data point outside the upper or lower process limits. As noted earlier in this chapter, the UPL and LPL predict with remarkable accuracy the range within which the next points will fall in a stable process that remains unchanged. A data point that falls outside these limits is a strong signal that the process has changed.

Figure 5-4 shows the data for the Vigo County Public Library's process "Register for a new adult library card" after the team made some improvements. Notice that one point toward the right-hand side is below the LPL. That point is a good example of pattern 1 and gave the team confidence that the change had affected the process in a positive way.

Pattern 2: Eight data points in a row above or below the average line in the X/SAMPLE graph. Eight or more points in a row that fall above or below the average on the process behavior chart is a clear indication that the process has changed.

After a year of improvement work in Lawrenceburg, the staff added data for the first quarter of 2004 (figure 5-5). They could quickly see that all twelve points in the X/SAMPLE graph were below the average (X_{AV}) from the year before, proof that their process had improved.

Other patterns. Several other patterns have been identified by leading statisticians; they are less predictive and more complicated, so we include them in a brief note.[3]

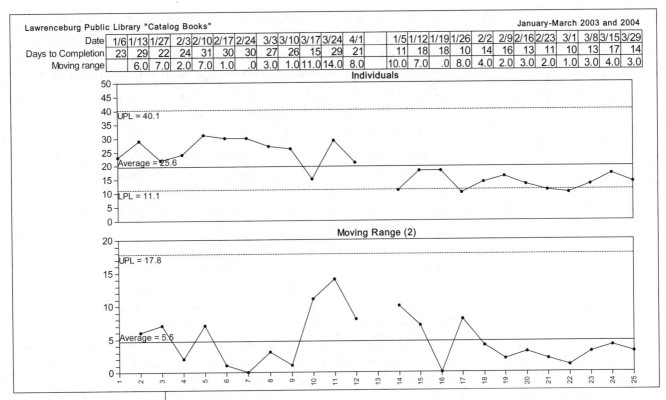

Lawrenceburg Public Library "Catalog Books"																								January-March 2003 and 2004
Date	1/6	1/13	1/27	2/3	2/10	2/17	2/24	3/3	3/10	3/17	3/24	4/1		1/5	1/12	1/19	1/26	2/2	2/9	2/16	2/23	3/1	3/8	3/15	3/29
Days to Completion	23	29	22	24	31	30	30	27	26	15	29	21		11	18	18	10	14	16	13	11	10	13	17	14
Moving range		6.0	7.0	2.0	7.0	1.0	.0	3.0	1.0	11.0	14.0	8.0		10.0	7.0	.0	8.0	4.0	2.0	3.0	2.0	1.0	3.0	4.0	3.0

Figure 5-5 Process behavior chart for "Catalog books," Lawrenceburg Public Library, with new set of data points.

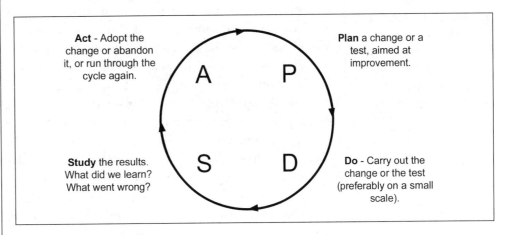

Figure 5-6 Shewhart PDSA cycle for learning and improvement.

What Change Can We Make That Will Result in Improvement?

Walter Shewhart and later W. Edwards Deming proposed that teams use an approach called the Plan-Do-Study-Act (PDSA) cycle (figure 5-6) to guide improvement efforts (see Deming 1986, 88; 1993, 135):

Plan: First the team must brainstorm and decide on an idea that might result in improvement. When a team is faced with the challenge of improving a process, the members can become very creative in conceiving ideas that might improve the process. They may revisit some of the "parking lot" ideas generated during the process mastering work. They may have gotten an idea from a customer, either external or internal. The process mastering may have suggested tasks to add, change, or delete.

Do: Next they try it—run an experiment on a trial basis. To be sure that the experiment is valid, they must inform everyone of the change, collect data, and plot new points on the process behavior chart.

Study: To see if the idea paid off in improvement, they study the process behavior chart. They know their experimental change was an improvement if the data show one of the patterns discussed above.

Act: If the process behavior chart shows that the process has been improved, the team modifies the process master to reflect the new "best-known way" to do the process. If the process is now at a point where the average and the variation are acceptable to the team and to customers, the team can begin work on another process. If the experiment improved the process but it still needs more improvement, the team can do another round of PDSA, brainstorming new ideas for improvement and trying them, then gathering data to verify whether the idea is causing improvement or not. If the changes do not result in improvement, the team reflects on what it learned, brainstorms new ideas for improvement, and goes around the PDSA cycle again.

This improvement approach is called rapid cycle improvement for good reason. The team does not need to spend weeks and months deliberating about what experiment to try. Team members just pick an idea and get on with it tomorrow. The faster data are gathered, the faster learning can take place. As soon as one PDSA cycle is complete, a second one can begin. The team will want to do this until it accomplishes the process improvement that it and customers desire.

If the process is an hourly or daily one, but the data the team is using are monthly or yearly, the cycle will take much longer than necessary. The team may be able to find a different measure that will allow it to plot at least one point daily.[4]

Trying improvements one at a time is the best way to be absolutely certain about the impact of each one. Rapid cycle improvement resembles the scientific method, beginning with a standardized process about which the team has data. Ideally, the team makes one alteration and continues to gather data. If the data indicate improvement, then the team knows its alteration was a good one and should be incorporated into the ongoing process master. If the team tries several things all at once, it cannot be sure which one caused the improvement. It might be that some that cause improvement are cancelled out by others that make the process worse.

Controlling the changes in order to test your hypotheses one at a time is especially important if some members of the team (or others in the library) are skeptical. If the change is the independent variable, while everything else remains the same, it is easier for everyone to acknowledge that this particular change caused the improvement.

Having said that, library teams are only people and sometimes they cannot wait to make changes. They have restrained themselves during the process mastering by adding ideas to their "parking lot." They have held back still longer while they gathered data. Sometimes the changes are so badly needed and so obvious that it just does not make sense to wait any longer. Many of the teams in the stories below tried several things and saw improvements.

Preliminary stats show that we are getting tons more business at the reference desk—so much so that we are back to double-staffing during certain hours.

—Maureen Lindstrom, E. B. Butler Library, University of Buffalo

Vigo County Public Library "Register for a New Adult Library Card"

In chapter 4 and earlier in this chapter, we described how the Vigo team created a process master and collected data. During their first rapid cycle improvement, they decided to try one of the ideas from their "parking lot"—a handout to describe the library's policies—and see if that would shorten the amount of time it took to give that information. When they plotted the data (figure 5-4), they saw the data point below the lower process limit, which provided clear evidence that the process had changed. The team figured a new average and process limits beginning with the first date after they implemented the handout (figure 5-7) and were pleased to discover that their changes had reduced the time for a customer to get a library card, as indicated by the lower average and smaller range between the higher and lower process limits.

Lawrenceburg Public Library "Catalog Books"

In chapter 4 we also wrote about the Lawrenceburg team's efforts to reduce the number of days for books from receipt to shelf-ready. Using the Plan-Do-Study-Act cycle between April 2003 and January 2004, they tried several improvements. They thought that some titles were sitting in the technical services area for a long time and driving up their average because they had given best sellers and titles on hold a priority, so they decided to handle each book in the order it was received instead. They thought that the variation in the number of shipments from one week to another could also be a factor and discovered

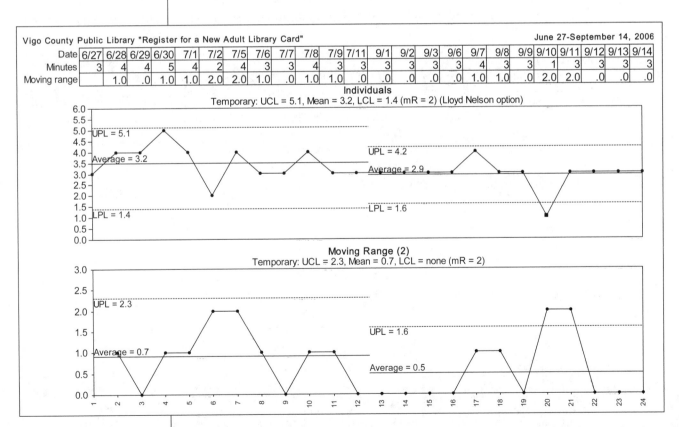

Figure 5-7   Process behavior chart for "Register for a new adult library card," Vigo County Public Library, showing recalculated averages and process limits following process improvement. Note slightly reduced average minutes as well as dramatic narrowing between UPL and LPL, indicating reduced variation.

that the acquisitions department had a practice of holding orders until a $1,000 total had been reached. They worked with the acquisitions staff to remove that limit and submit each order as it was completed. Finally, they knew that sometimes a boxful of books would get misdirected on the loading dock, so they asked their UPS delivery driver to bring their boxes right to their second-floor work area. Their process behavior chart at the end of the first quarter of 2004 proved that the process had improved (figure 5-5), so they refigured the average and process limits, as shown in figure 5-8.

Michigan City Public Library "Shelve Audiovisual Materials"

The Michigan City process improvement team knew that it was difficult to shelve audiovisual materials, since each format had different shelving rules. Their data showed that, on average, more than six hundred audiovisual items per month were misshelved. They created a flowchart and held a training session for all the shelvers. For the next three months, the misshelved total dropped, until it finally settled into an average less than four hundred. The team was pleased with the improvement but went back to work to get additional reductions. Figure 5-9 shows the average before the process mastering and a new average computed after it. Notice that the last seven points are at or below the new average. Whatever they're trying appears to be working. In one more month, they can be sure.

Benton County Public Library "Handle Packages"

The story was a little different at the Benton County Public Library. The director felt that sending and receiving packages through the statewide courier was taking more and

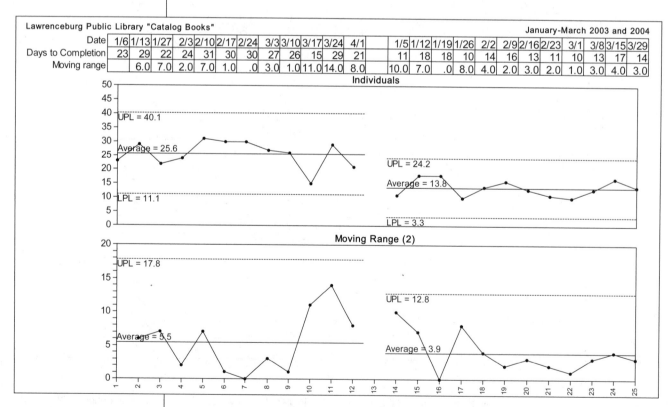

Figure 5-8 Process behavior chart for "Catalog books," Lawrenceburg Public Library, showing recalculated averages and process limits following the first round of process improvement. Note lower average and reduced variation.

Month	1	2	3	4	5	6	7	8	9	10	11	12	1	2	3	4	5	6	7	8	9	10	11	12
Items Misshelved	615	580	650	680	600	575	590	630	655	610	640	660	620	550	450	400	390	350	370	360	340	375	350	340
Moving range		35.0	70.0	30.0	80.0	25.0	15.0	40.0	25.0	45.0	30.0	20.0	40.0	70.0	100.0	50.0	10.0	40.0	20.0	10.0	20.0	35.0	25.0	10.0

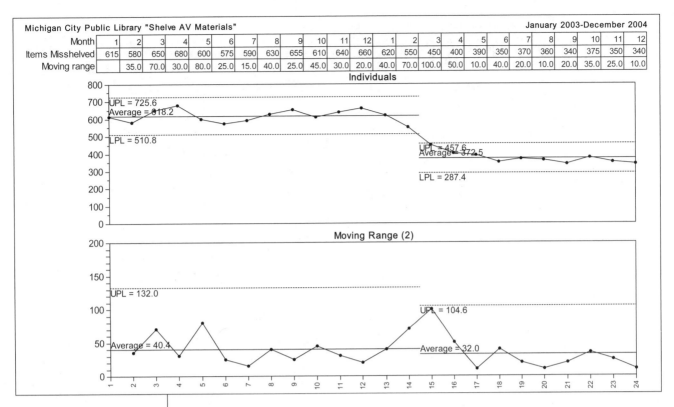

Figure 5-9   Process behavior chart for "Shelve AV materials," Michigan City Public Library, showing reduced average items misshelved after process changes.

more of her time. She discovered that she had two years' worth of data about packages sent and received, which she combined to use for plotting, since both sending and receiving took time. Her process behavior chart (figure 5-10) showed a steady upward trend. When we asked her what was going on, she didn't know. When we showed the data to another library director, whose library also participated in the same shared automation system, she said, "Oh, I know why. Our shared catalog became available via the Internet in July 2001." When we recalculated the average and process behavior limits for each of those periods (figure 5-11), it became obvious that making the catalog accessible via the Internet changed the process of package handling at Benton County—and probably at the other forty participating libraries. The new average was nearly twice that of the old. Looking at the data, the director could predict that the increased traffic would continue. She could report to her board that the work and expense of making the catalog more available were making it easier for the library's customers to see the holdings in the shared catalog and take advantage of borrowing them.

Mooresville Public Library "Discharge Books"

The Mooresville Public Library was troubled by the number of books that made it back to the shelves without being properly discharged. Every time this happened, a customer received an unnecessary overdue notice, which frequently led to upset customers and extra trips to the shelves by the staff to search for books. The library's reputation for accuracy suffered. The staff tracked how many discharge errors they found in a month. After several months, they averaged more than twenty per month. They brainstormed about what they could do to improve this situation. They suspected that the location of the carts might be part of the problem and tried something different. They moved the cart for

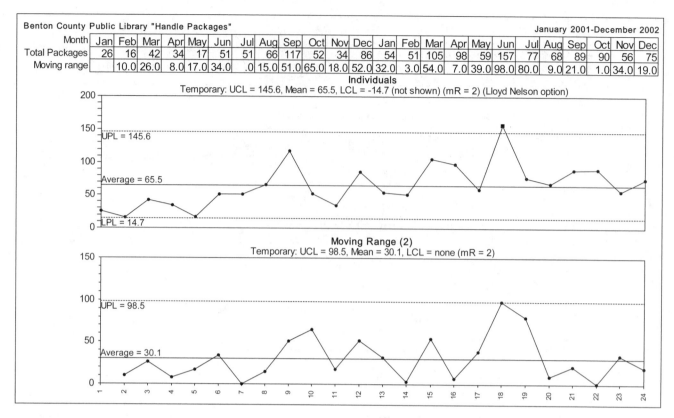

Month	Jan	Feb	Mar	Apr	May	Jun	Jul	Aug	Sep	Oct	Nov	Dec	Jan	Feb	Mar	Apr	May	Jun	Jul	Aug	Sep	Oct	Nov	Dec
Total Packages	26	16	42	34	17	51	51	66	117	52	34	86	54	51	105	98	59	157	77	68	89	90	56	75
Moving range		10.0	26.0	8.0	17.0	34.0	.0	15.0	51.0	65.0	18.0	52.0	32.0	3.0	54.0	7.0	39.0	98.0	80.0	9.0	21.0	1.0	34.0	19.0

Figure 5-10 Process behavior chart for "Handle packages," Benton County Public Library.

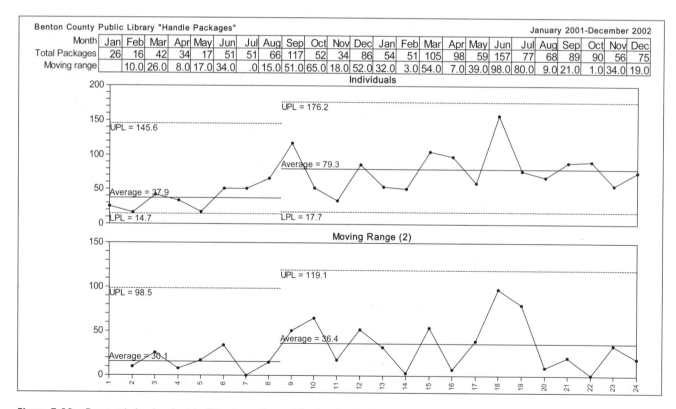

Month	Jan	Feb	Mar	Apr	May	Jun	Jul	Aug	Sep	Oct	Nov	Dec	Jan	Feb	Mar	Apr	May	Jun	Jul	Aug	Sep	Oct	Nov	Dec
Total Packages	26	16	42	34	17	51	51	66	117	52	34	86	54	51	105	98	59	157	77	68	89	90	56	75
Moving range		10.0	26.0	8.0	17.0	34.0	.0	15.0	51.0	65.0	18.0	52.0	32.0	3.0	54.0	7.0	39.0	98.0	80.0	9.0	21.0	1.0	34.0	19.0

Figure 5-11 Process behavior chart for "Handle packages," Benton County Public Library, showing increased average number of packages handled following change in shared catalog in August. Note that variation also increased.

discharged books further behind the circulation desk, so that patrons would be less likely to put a newly returned book there. They painted the two discharge carts—red (stop!) for the one with books not yet discharged, and green (go!) for the one where they put discharged books ready to shelve. They also wondered whether their automated system was catching every discharge, so they decided to do the discharge procedure twice. They trained the entire staff on the new process. Within the first month, the number of errors dropped. After seven months, they recomputed the average and found that it was fewer than four errors—an 80 percent reduction (figure 5-12).

Cazenovia College "Instruct First-Year Students in Library Use"

The Cazenovia College Library was interested in demonstrating outcomes from its freshman bibliographic instruction efforts. During September each year, the library presents a twenty-minute, formal bibliographic instruction session to each first-year seminar class, using specific pathfinders for each class, developed in cooperation with the instructor and including directions on how to locate books, journal articles, and websites for the class's topic. In October or November, instructors administer the "General Library Knowledge Survey." The reference staff scores each survey and returns results to the faculty, who can then return results to each student. The survey also includes several comment areas in which students can express their thoughts about the library instruction and other perceptions about library services. Between 2004 and 2005, the percentage of students passing increased from just over 60 percent to more than 90 percent, and the variation was reduced considerably (figure 5-13). The library attributed the increases to closer working

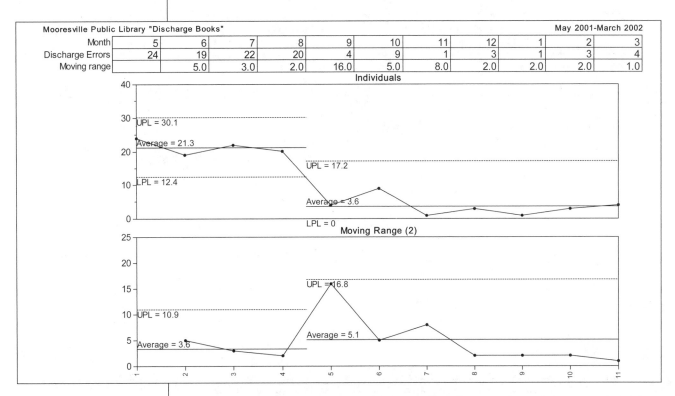

Figure 5-12 Process behavior chart for "Discharge books," Mooresville Public Library, showing improvement after process change. Note that average discharge errors were reduced while variation increased, at least initially. This may have resulted from incomplete training during the improvement, because the last four points on the moving range chart are below the average.

relationships with faculty and to its upgrade to new integrated library software, which allowed unlimited remote access to databases and e-books for students and faculty.

Step 5.4
Does the process meet expectations?

This is a critical decision point for the process improvement team. Three different conditions are possible:

Condition A: The data on the process behavior chart show that the change in the process is an improvement by exhibiting one of the patterns described under step 5.3. If one of these patterns is present, then the team must ask, is the improvement enough to meet the customer's and the library's needs and expectations? If the answer is yes, the team completes the work of making the change in the process master and distributes it.

Condition B: If the data on the process behavior chart show that the process change resulted in improvement, but that more improvement is needed, the team returns to the beginning of the PDSA cycle and experiments with another possible process improvement.

Condition C: If the data on the process behavior chart show that the process change did not result in improvement, the team returns to the beginning of the PDSA

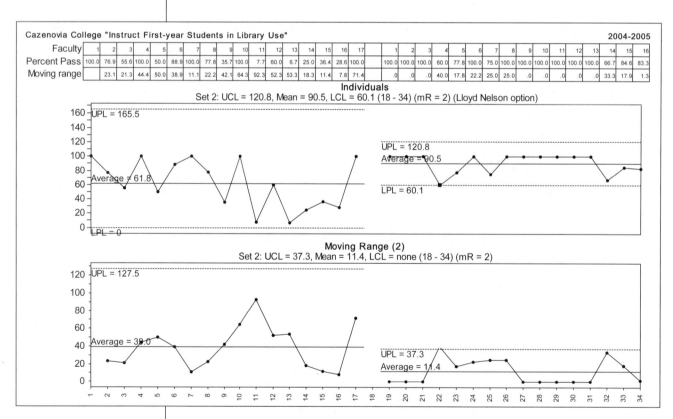

Figure 5-13 Process behavior chart for "Instruct first-year students in library use," Cazenovia College Library. The average passing rate has increased following the process change, and variation is reduced.

cycle to try another experiment. The fact that the process was not improved is not viewed as a failure, but as a learning experience. The team has more information and can try another experiment.

In many cases, it takes a team several PDSA cycles before the process has reached a level of quality acceptable to external and internal customers. In fact, it is often quite amazing how much improvement is possible once a team puts its collective creativity and knowledge of the process to work.

Step 5.5
Maintain the new level of quality in the process.

It may take several rounds of rapid cycle improvement over a few weeks before a team is satisfied that its process is stable, performing well, and meeting customer expectations. When the process has reached this level of performance, the team makes revisions to the process master reflecting the new tasks and then disbands. The team members (or others in a new team) are now free to work on the next process that needs improvement.

The process owner continues to plot data points to see that the process remains stable at its new level of performance. The process owner uses the process master to train new employees. The process master is also available for other process owners to consult as they are mastering their processes and improving them.

Is the library finished improving? Probably not. The experience of improving the first process usually unleashes a chain reaction. The team probably left lots of ideas for improving this and other processes on its "parking lot." Team members talking to customers and suppliers may have discovered other processes surrounding their process that could also use attention. With their increased awareness of processes and customer needs in general, they may have noticed new areas for attention. They may want to try the tools they used again. They may realize they have been collecting data that could be put to use in studying and improving another process.

The leaders with whom we have worked have described this blossoming. One director reported that so many staff members were coming to her asking for charters to improve processes that she had to impose a moratorium on issuing new charters so that improvement efforts in one area didn't interfere with those in another, and so that the staff could still cover their routine duties.

CONCLUSION

In this chapter you created a process behavior chart by completing some straightforward statistical calculations and adding them to the run chart.

You studied the process behavior chart, which helped answer several important questions:

- Is the process in control or out of control?
- Is there a great deal of variation?
- Is the average higher or lower than customers expect?
- Is the process getting better, getting worse, or staying the same?
- Does the process go through cycles?

After studying the process behavior chart, your team more than likely discovered room for improvement—in the average, in the variation, or in both. If you did, your next step was to charter a team to improve the process—and soon.

Three questions guided your rapid cycle improvement process: What are we trying to do? How will we know if a change is an improvement? What change can we make that will result in an improvement?

You selected an improvement idea and tested it, plotting points on your process behavior chart and analyzing them for evidence of improvement. You plotted enough points to know whether the idea led to improvement or not. If it did, you incorporated the change into the process master. If the change made enough improvement to meet your own and customers' expectations, you made plans to monitor the process and are ready to move on to a new process. If the change did not improve the process, or if there was still room for improvement, you went back through the PDSA cycle again, choosing another idea to test and plotting more points until you found a change that improved the process.

In chapter 6 you learn how to extend process improvement throughout the library and how to manage in this new kind of workplace, where the focus is always on improving processes to please customers.

NOTES

1. The process behavior chart was originally referred to as a control chart by Walter Shewhart (1931). Donald J. Wheeler coined the term "process behavior chart" in 2003 (2003, 97). There are several kinds of process behavior charts. In this volume we use the most common, the X and moving range chart. For more information on these and other types of process behavior charts, see Wheeler and Chambers (1992).

2. Caution: Teams sometimes take on a life of their own. Some have been known to go on for years. Many times teams lose their way. It is important to emphasize what is expected and pay close attention to the monitoring aspect of the charter.

3. Other patterns of process change have also been identified by statisticians, including Wheeler (2003, 111). The following patterns require more calculation and are used less frequently:

    Pattern 3: Successive points in the upper or lower quarter within the process limits in the X/SAMPLE chart. The process has changed if three out of four successive data points fall in the upper or lower 25 percent of the area between the process limits. To find the line delineating the upper and lower 25 percent of the X chart, subtract the difference between the UPL and the average and divide that number by 2. Add the resulting number to the average for the upper quartile line and subtract that number from the average to get the lower quartile line.

    Pattern 4: Data points more than two standard deviations above or below the average on the X/SAMPLE chart. To meet this standard, two of three successive points must be at least two standard deviations above or below the average. To determine the line two standard deviations above or below the average, simply add or subtract two standard deviations ($2 \times S$), applying the S value used in your process behavior chart calculations.

    Pattern 5: Data points within one standard deviation of the average. When four out of five successive data points fall within one standard deviation above or below the average on the X/SAMPLE chart, the process has changed.

    Pattern 6: Seven or more points increasing or decreasing in a row on an X/SAMPLE chart. This pattern has been mentioned in the continuous improvement literature, but, according to Wheeler, "Many people have been taught to use a rule for six or seven points going up or down. This rule has repeatedly been found to be of little use except to increase the number of false alarms. It should not be used" (1992, 111).

4. There are some circumstances that make it impossible to collect data rapidly; perhaps the process is completed only once a year (e.g., subscribing to a database) or even less frequently (e.g., hiring a consultant). In such cases, the team can work on other processes at the same time.

Chapter 6 | Manage Process Improvement throughout the Library System

Launching an effort to improve processes in a library—or a department, branch, or initiative of the library—is not a trivial matter. Usually the leadership of the library initiates such an effort either because the library is already pretty good and wants to get significantly better or because it is in a crisis and needs to do something to turn itself around. In either case, library leaders must understand the commitment they are making.

Ideally the leaders are the library's top administrators. Managers of departments, branches, or teams may lead process improvement in the areas they manage, but without support from administrators their efforts may not achieve lasting results.

ENSURING LEADERSHIP COMMITMENT

The most important ingredient to ensure success of process improvement is for leadership to participate in the effort. Conversely, the surest way to kill the effort is for leaders to kick off the effort with great fanfare and then walk away from it. Process improvement can change everything by engaging teams in pleasing customers, but it won't happen without the high expectations, support, and participation of the library's leadership.

For leaders, there is a delicate balance between having high expectations and having patience while teams learn and try out their own improvement ideas. The work may seem painfully slow at first. Initial efforts may not yield startling improvements. But with adequate time, tools, and coaching, teams deepen their understanding of customer needs and of the processes.

Meanwhile, leaders have four important roles: modeling, providing support, spreading process improvement throughout the organization, and building governance support.

Leaders *model process improvement* by

- leading the training or at least participating in the training
- leading or participating on a team
- making decisions using data
- putting "progress on the process improvement initiative" at the top of the agenda at each staff meeting
- employing process improvement tools at every opportunity
- focusing on customer feedback in choosing processes to improve
- being persistent and planning to do it for the rest of their lives, learning as they go

> *The continuous improvement methodology has changed the entire climate of our library system for the better. It has been enormously helpful in boosting morale, unifying purpose, spirit, and attitude among staff in all departments and both facilities.*
>
> —Sally Stegner, Lawrenceburg (IN) Public Library

Leaders *provide support (and a little pressure) for process improvement* by

- empowering teams to make real change
- having high expectations of results
- ensuring that nothing interferes with the time set aside to work on process improvement
- being alert for just-in-time training and professional development opportunities as the teams and individuals encounter difficulties
- taking a sincere interest in what each team is doing
- keeping the pressure on by requesting regular reports
- communicating and celebrating process improvement successes
- spending more time managing the processes than managing the people
- breaking down barriers between departments
- managing the whole effort from an overall system perspective

Leaders *help spread process improvement throughout the library* by

- understanding that process standardization and improvement through employee empowerment is the new way of doing business—it is a big step!
- insisting on having an owner for every process
- reinforcing the concept that all processes have suppliers who must meet expectations and customers who must be surprised and delighted—even within the library
- insisting on having at least one measurement for each process
- involving *all* staff in the effort
- gearing up to manage the entire effort and being prepared for the enthusiasm, energy, and creativity that is unleashed when employees are truly empowered

Leaders *build governance (board or other entity) support* by

- offering an overview of continuous improvement or opportunities for more board training
- keeping the board informed about process improvement efforts and successes
- helping the board or governing entity standardize and improve its own processes

COORDINATING PROCESS IMPROVEMENT EFFORTS ACROSS THE LIBRARY

In chapter 5 we described using the Plan-Do-Study-Act (PDSA) cycle as the basic methodology for improving a process. The intent is for the improvement team to go around that cycle numerous times until the process is very good and predictable. But that is only one team working on one process. In a library committed to process improvement, numerous process improvement teams are simultaneously going around the PDSA cycle, improving their processes and steadily advancing toward the library's goal. Figure 6-1 shows several process improvement teams, each working through PDSA cycles. As each process improves, it rises along a ramp toward the goal. It is the library leadership's job to choose and to manage the ramps leading to the goal.

Even the most mundane work can be given meaning and value for those who perform it if they understand how it benefits, even in the simplest of ways, the lives of others. Process-centered work can help satisfy everyone's hunger for connection with something beyond themselves and their own needs. It widens our horizons and connects us with others—with our teammates, with our organization, with our customers. In the process-centered world dignity is restored to work, the dignity that was lost to workers who only performed repetitive tasks.
—Michael Hammer (1996, 268)

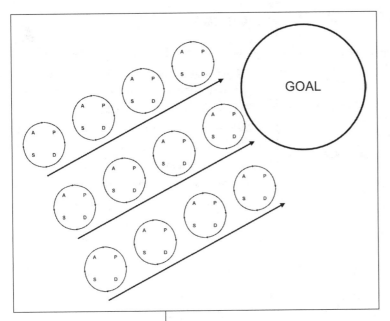

Figure 6-1 Sequential and concurrent PDSA cycles result in steady improvement toward a single organizational goal.

In preceding chapters we focused on standardizing, gathering data for, and improving a single process. As more and more teams are engaged in process mastering and improvement, the library leadership may decide to formalize its own processes for choosing processes for improvement and managing improvement efforts.

LIBRARY-WIDE STEERING GROUP

As process improvement expands, most libraries find it advantageous to form a steering group to lead the process mastering and continuous improvement effort. After the culture of continuous improvement becomes routine (in perhaps several years), the library will probably choose to incorporate the steering group's work as the new normal work of supervisors. The steering group represents various areas in the library. Individuals asked to serve on steering groups must have leadership abilities, respect from and for other staff members, awareness of the interaction of several processes in the library, enthusiasm to want to change things for the better, and energy. They are likely to be the "thought leaders" in the library and the busy people you go to when you really need to get something done.

Following the same approach used to give authority to a single process mastering team, the steering group receives a charter from the director, which might look something like figure 6-2.

Step 6.1
Prioritize development of process masters.

One of the first things a steering group must do is decide the processes on which to work. There are four approaches to choosing processes for improvement:

1. Choose processes that support accomplishment of the strategic plan's key success factors. This is the formal approach outlined in chapter 2.

2. Choose processes that have the potential of increasing customer satisfaction. They may be the focus of frequent customer complaints or those that surveys or observations suggest will surprise and delight customers.

3. Choose processes that cause staff complaints and frustration. Staff members know the daily frustrations, and they have ideas about how to make processes better.

4. Choose processes that seem to result in errors, mistakes, or waste.

From the "lean management" literature come eight areas that offer great opportunities for improvement:[1]

Date	
To	Continuous Improvement Steering Committee
From	Director
Purpose	Initiate and guide the library's continuous improvement.
Expected results	Standardized and improved library processes, Improved customer satisfaction, Reduction in waste, and Empowered employees.
Authority	To form teams to standardize and improve processes. To provide training in process mastering and rapid cycle improvement. To manage process master development and process improvement. To involve employees in up to two hours per week in this continuous improvement work.
Limitations	Don't fail to: Have a logical plan for which processes will be worked on and in what order. Keep employees on track and productive in their meeting time. Involve all employees. Make all process masters available to all staff and see that they are followed. Keep all process masters up to date with the latest changes.
Reporting	A quarterly written report indicating: Number of processes mastered. Number of rapid cycle improvement cycles completed. Indications or measurements of increased customer satisfaction. Indications or measurements of waste reduction.

Figure 6-2 Sample charter for a continuous improvement steering committee.

Distance

This waste is related to moving things—books, files, supplies. It occurs because of poor workplace layout, poor workflow, and inefficient location of suppliers to processes and customers of processes. Obviously items must be moved, but the goal is to reduce this necessary waste.

Excess Motion

In addition to the time lost, wasted human motion—unnecessary reaching, twisting, bending, and walking—leads to injuries and accidents.

One library with which we worked had a Friends of the Library book sale in the lobby of the library every week. The Friends volunteers, many of them in their seventies and eighties, had to haul the heavy boxes of books out of the storage room in the morning and back at the end of the day. In the first rapid cycle improvement, the library director noticed and gave the Friends some old book carts. A few months later, the library moved the sale into a dedicated space in the library, where the Friends could store and sort the books and simply unlock the door for sales. Since volunteers could sort and run the store at the same time, they were able to expand their open hours, resulting in more sales.

Waiting/Delay

This waste occurs when workers or machines wait for work. Delays happen for various reasons, such as waiting for materials, waiting for a decision, waiting for a problem to be cleared up.

In libraries, some of the waiting is done by staff. What about, for instance, reference librarians who have no customers to serve when they are on the desk?

Some of the waiting is done by customers, who wait for materials to be ordered, prepared, and finally shelved. Some of the waiting is done by the materials—think of those high-demand items on hold that wait to be picked up, or those that wait over the weekend in the book drop or wait several hours to be checked in and reshelved.

From the library world, four examples were suggested by employees: borrowing an item on interlibrary loan from a distant library rather than from another branch on the same campus; handcarting boxes of books from the mailroom located at the other end of the building from the technical services department; helping a customer find items in the stacks, which are located at the opposite end of the department (or on another floor); and sending all the materials ordered by a library in one city through an acquisitions department in another city.

Defects/Errors

All the cost associated with making and correcting defective products or services is a waste. This includes the material, time, energy, and distraction associated with resolving the problem. In libraries, this waste might show up in ineffective meetings and programs, poor bindings, lost items, having to make apologies, or personnel counseling. Defects are often caused by nonstandard work processes or underutilization of employees' skills.

Defects may also be present when inputs are delivered to the library. For example, a library with which we worked was involved in a major renovation and addition, so the library had moved to temporary quarters. In the final stages of preparing to reopen, the contractor had installed 60 percent of the shelving before the library decided to reject it because large flakes of paint were already peeling off. The contractor had to disassemble the shelving, remove it, and reorder shelving to replace it—all at the supplier's cost. Because it was the supplier's busy season, the library had to delay its reopening and pay rent in its temporary quarters for several additional months.

Excess Inventory

This waste relates to keeping unnecessary staff, supplies, books, or other materials. Libraries are often guilty of not culling unused books, old pieces of equipment, or furniture that just take up space.

Some examples supplied by library staff: keeping empty boxes in the back room "just in case"; buying four million 3M exit strips; storing a whole shelf full of book pockets, which the library has not used in years; and stacking boxes of ALA interlibrary loan forms.

Overprocessing

This is a subtle form of waste that relates to overdesign, or giving customers more than they value.

One example: A library was open Monday through Thursday until 9:00 p.m., staffed by three reference librarians. The staff perceived that usage was low on Thursday evenings. They gathered data and were surprised to learn that use of the library was equally slow every night.

Overproduction

This waste deals with providing products or services that are not valued by customers. Taiichi Ohno, father of the Toyota production system, said that overproduction was the root of all manufacturing evil (Ohno 1988). It is the worst waste because it includes all the other wastes.

Several examples of overproduction have been suggested by library employees: Eight employees share a single, rigid job description; most times, two are sitting quietly in their cubicles, waiting for work to do. The library purchases and maintains warehouses full of infrequently used bound journals when the full text is available for a fee online. An employee counts the cash in the cash drawer at the end of the day before putting it in the safe; the next morning the same employee counts the money again. Because the library does not know its customers, it occasionally purchases and stores materials that no one ever uses.

Knowledge Disconnection

This occurs when there are disconnects within the library or between the library and its customers and suppliers. Disconnects within the library can be horizontal, vertical, or temporal. These inhibit the flow of knowledge, ideas, and creativity, causing frustration, missed opportunities, and lack of a shared vision of the future.

One library realized that it had thirteen methods of communication and that staff did not always use a method that was appropriate to the circumstance. Gossip within the library is a classic example of knowledge disconnection. Some supervisors do not pass information on to employees because it is a source of power.

Step 6.2
Manage and support the development of initial process masters.

Once an initial batch of processes is selected for improvement, the steering group needs a plan for initially developing the process masters. See the step-by-step approach below and in the deployment flowchart in figure 6-3. Those involved (shown across the top) are the process master administrator, the steering group/sponsor, the team leader/process owner, and the teams. The rounded boxes in the flowchart indicate primary responsibility; the circles indicate participation or consultation.

Step 6.2.1   Charter teams.

This step involves writing a charter for the team and passing it to the team leader and the team, as described in chapter 3.

Step 6.2.2   Develop process master and report to steering group.

As teams standardize their processes using the process master approach discussed in chapter 3, each team reports regularly to the steering group on its progress. To spread the workload, individual members of the steering group may act as sponsors for individual teams, and thus each process progress report can be sent to and monitored by only one person.

The reports to the steering group allow it to monitor progress of the teams and to provide encouragement and support. Steering group members' responses are offered in the spirit of coaching. They may suggest use of another tool, offer a resource, help resolve a problem, or ask a question to provoke thought. They never meddle or criticize.

Our whole staff has gotten involved in process management and problem solving.
—Lynn Jurewicz, Mooresville (IN) Public Library

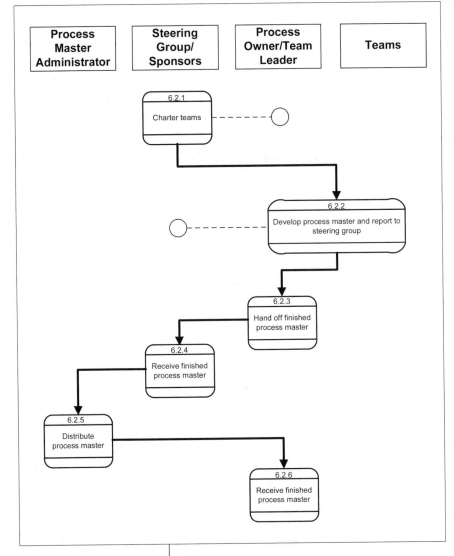

Process Master Administrator	Steering Group/ Sponsors	Process Owner/Team Leader	Teams

Figure 6-3 Deployment flowchart showing steps and responsibilities for managing and supporting development of initial process masters.

Step 6.2.3 *Hand off finished process master.*

This step corresponds to step 3.9 (Sign on and take responsibility) in chapter 3. Here the team reports to the steering group that it has completed the process master and agreed upon the "best-known way," and that it is turning the finished process master over to the process owner.

Step 6.2.4 *Receive finished process master.*

The steering group receives the completed work and makes sure that the process master is turned over to the process master administrator, a single staff member who may or may not be a member of the steering group. The process master administrator's job is to serve as a repository for the official completed process masters and to record updates to process masters as they are changed and improved. As the library completes more and more process masters, this job becomes critically important.

Before adding the process master, the process master administrator makes sure that the document is complete and in the standard format adopted by the library. Each process master includes a flowchart, customer and supplier screens, key tasks worksheets, measures, and a list of tools, equipment, and supplies. The process master administrator prepares the process master (or oversees its preparation) for distribution to others in the library.

Step 6.2.5 *Distribute process master.*

For many libraries, the best way to distribute the process master to all staff is to make it available on the library's intranet. There may also be print copies at the locations where the processes are done, so that staff can easily refer to them. We have seen the process masters for circulation, for example, in a binder at the circulation desk. We have seen flowcharts laminated and mounted on the wall. We have also seen them on the intranet only.

Step 6.2.6   ***Receive finished process master.***

Every process must have a person designated as the process owner. This may well be the process master team leader or the supervisor of the process, but it could also be someone who works with the process regularly. The process owner receives the finished process master and is responsible for seeing that everyone follows it until a better method is found.

FINDING TIME FOR PROCESS IMPROVEMENT

Library employees, managers, and directors are already busy. Where will they get the extra time to invest in process improvement work? The answer is, *this is the new way of working.* An initial investment in learning how to do process improvement and in improving the first processes is required, of course. It feels like extra work. It is hard to find time. The team faces many uncertainties as it tries new tools and discovers from the data that the process is not perfect. But it is just that—an investment. As processes are mastered and improved, there will be much less time spent fixing things that didn't go right the first time.

The question that directors and team members routinely ask at the beginning of their process improvement efforts is, how long does it take? We'll answer in two ways:

How much time does it take to master a process? Plan on about eight hours for a team to complete a process master. It may take a little longer the first time as team members get comfortable working together and learn the language and tools. After the first or second effort, they should be able to complete a process master in six to eight hours. Weekly two-hour meetings are ideal, long enough for the team to get a significant amount of work done and short enough that team members can maintain their focus.

How much time should we devote as a library? To answer this question, let's return to the idea of waste. In numerous workshops and training sessions, we have asked librarians how much of their time, on a routine daily basis, is wasted fixing things that didn't go right the first time. On average, participants estimate that 30 percent of their time is wasted. That is twelve hours in a standard forty-hour workweek. It turns out that libraries are no different from other organizations, according to quality consultant Joseph Juran, who studied numerous organizations for many years (see Godfrey 2007).

If all employees are involved in mastering and improving processes and spend two hours of the twelve that are wasted each week in mastering and improving processes, and if all employees are involved on teams of four or five individuals, the library can expect to standardize and improve at least one process for each employee in the library in a year's time. For instance, if a library has twenty-four full-time employees, and each of them participates on a team of four, investing two hours a week over four weeks to master a process, that is six processes mastered in one month. Add two more months to complete the rapid cycle improvements, and in one quarter six processes have been improved. In the next three quarters eighteen more processes will be improved, resulting in an annual total of twenty-four processes improved. By this point, rather than taking extra time, the improved processes will have reduced so many errors, eliminated so much rework, and reduced such substantial waste that the library will have plenty of time to invest in accelerating the improvement and in serving its customers better.

Step 6.3
Manage second- and subsequent-generation process changes.

When a team has tested a change and found that it resulted in measurable improvement, it is time to update the process master to reflect the revised process. We know that whenever anything changes in a system it affects everything else in the system, so changes in individual processes must be evaluated against the effects they may cause elsewhere. Therefore, consideration of the proposed change must be communicated.

Figure 6-4 is a deployment flowchart of the participants and steps to be considered when managing process master changes. Each steering group may want to modify and adapt the flowchart to fit its needs. The flowchart outlines a communication scheme and an approval process for process changes. A diamond-shaped decision box indicates a point where the answer to a yes-or-no question determines the next step.

Step 6.3.1 Team (or individual) sends recommended process change to process owner.

Ideas for improving processes may come from the process improvement team, which sends the recommended change to the process owner. Figure 6-4 shows the steps through which an idea coming from a team must pass.

Sometimes, individuals outside the team (staff or customers) may have an idea for improving a process. If the individual is a member of the process improvement team, he/she may add the idea to the "parking lot" or bring it up for team consideration. The process owner may ask the individual to provide some data that demonstrate the need for the change. If the individual has the data, the process owner may invite him/her to present the idea to the team; if not, the process owner may suggest that he/she gather data first.

If the idea is coming from a customer, the process owner and team should discuss it and decide whether they have any relevant data or need to gather some. If the data support the change, the team proceeds with the next steps.

Step 6.3.2 Process owner sends notice of proposed change to other process owners.

The process owner sends a notice of the proposed change to all other process owners. At first this might appear daunting, but it can be a simple e-mail notification stating the change and asking for a response only if the recipient thinks the change may adversely affect his/her process.

Step 6.3.3 Other process owners distribute proposed change for comments.

The other process owners notify people working in their processes of the proposed change and solicit their concerns, if any.

Step 6.3.4 Other process team members comment on proposed change.

After considering the change, process team members send their concerns, if any, back to their process owners.

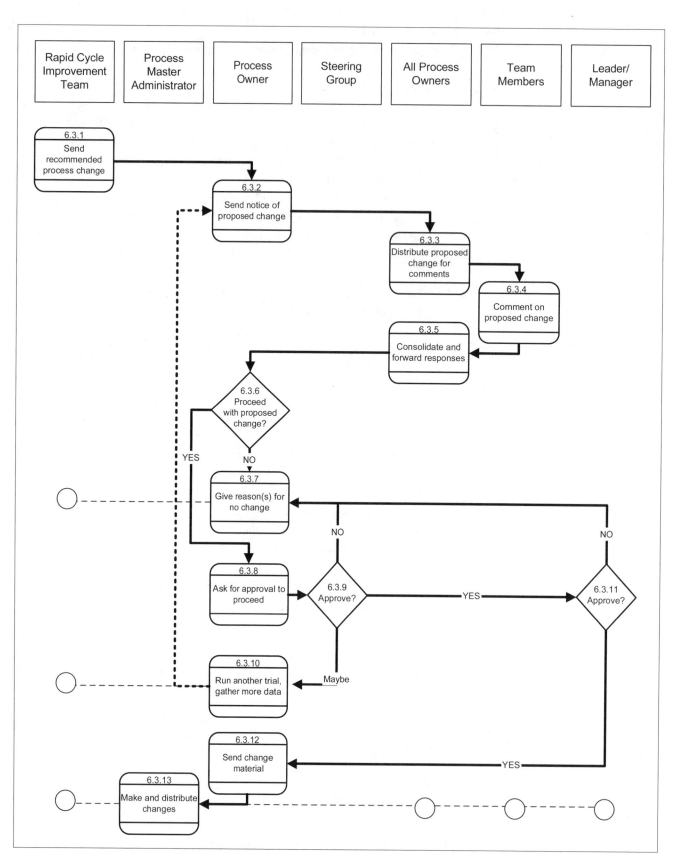

Figure 6-4 Deployment flowchart showing steps and responsibilities for managing second- and subsequent-generation process master changes.

Step 6.3.5 Other process owners consolidate and forward responses to process owner.

The process owners consolidate and clarify any responses from their team members and forward them on to the originating process owner.

Step 6.3.6 Process owner proceeds with or rejects proposed change.

Based on responses from others, the process owner decides whether to proceed with the change or not. If the decision is to make no change, the process owner goes to step 6.3.7. If the decision is to proceed with the change, the process owner goes to step 6.3.8.

Step 6.3.7 If no change, process owner gives reasons to rapid cycle improvement team.

The process owner gives feedback to the team or individual(s) who suggested the change to explain why the change cannot be made. This is an important step and must not be overlooked.

Step 6.3.8 If change, process owner asks steering group for approval to proceed.

If the decision is to proceed with the change, the process owner seeks approval to make the change from the steering group.

Step 6.3.9 Steering group makes decision.

The steering group has three choices. (1) It can reject the proposed change and send the reasons for disapproval back to the process owner, who then informs folks that the change was rejected and why (step 6.3.7). (2) It can approve the proposed process change and send a recommendation to management to approve the process change (step 6.3.11). (3) It can ask for more data (step 6.3.10). In this case the process owner is asked to have those proposing the change gather more data to provide evidence that this is a correct change to make, which sends the change back to the team.

Step 6.3.10 Run another trial and gather more data.

If the steering group wants to see more evidence that the change is warranted, they may ask for more data or further rapid cycle improvement. It is incumbent on the team or individuals who initiated the change request to provide what the steering group asks for.

Step 6.3.11 Leadership makes decision.

The culture and leadership of organizations vary. In some organizations, employees and supervisors are given great autonomy. For example, the steering group could be authorized to give approvals for all process changes. If this is the case, this step can be eliminated. In other organizations, the top leaders want to pass judgment on things like process changes. They can disapprove the change and inform the process owner, who in turn informs those who proposed the change (step 6.3.7). If leaders approve the change, they inform the steering group and process owner (step 6.3.12).

Step 6.3.12 *Process owner sends change material to process administrator.*

When all the communication and all the approvals are complete, the process owner provides material to the process master administrator to have the process master updated to the latest version. Usually all that is changed is the flowchart, key tasks worksheet, or both. One way of communicating the changes to the administrator is to mark the changes on a copy of the existing process master.

Step 6.3.13 *Process administrator makes and distributes changes.*

The changes provided by the process owner are made to the process master record. Through the chosen method of communicating information about process masters, the administrator notifies everyone that a process has been updated. The administrator should have some form of document control to archive old versions and make sure that people are using the latest version. Note that, if the library is using paper copies of the process master, there must be a plan to replace the existing copies with new ones so everyone is working from the latest version.

COMPUTER SOFTWARE FOR PROCESS MASTERING

Once a team or an entire library gets into process standardization and improvement, it begins to realize that appropriate computer software is very helpful. This is an ever-evolving area, but we can offer the following suggestions for the near term.

Flowcharts. The flowcharts in this book were created with Microsoft Visio software specifically developed for flowcharting. Documents produced in Visio can be shared with others who have Visio software or saved as PDF files for distribution to those who do not.

Flowcharts can also be drawn in Microsoft Word, Excel, or PowerPoint. There are numerous other free or commercial flowcharting programs, such as SmartDraw, EDraw Flowchart Software, RFFlow, Quickie Flowcharts, and Novagraph Chartist. For larger libraries, iGrafx (www.iGrafx.com) offers Flowcharter for creating flowcharts, cause and effect diagrams, Gantt chart, and other project management visuals.

If the flowcharts are maintained in the computer network, hyperlinks can be inserted into the flowchart tasks to take a user to the key tasks worksheet for more detail or to other documents such as forms that must be filled out, other process flowcharts, pictures, or even videos showing someone doing a task.

Customer and supplier screens. The best tool we have discovered for creating customer and supplier screens is Microsoft Excel. Customer and supplier screen templates are available for downloading at www.rwwilson.com.

Key tasks worksheet. The key tasks worksheet can be set up as a table or as a spreadsheet, with pictures or hyperlinks inserted.

Process behavior charts. W. Edwards Deming was known for asking the question, "What do great men [we substitute "librarians"] do?" The answer he always gave was, "Plot points!" By this he meant that plotting points with a pencil was quite adequate for learning about a process.

You can, and believe it or not probably should, initially do this by hand. There is certainly something powerful and enlightening that results from hand calculating and plotting the data. In particular it avoids the "if it comes out of the computer, it must be right" syndrome. These days, however, we like our graphs to be pretty, neat, and colorful. And if there are a lot of data points, it is tedious to do the arithmetic associated with calculating averages and process limits, so numerous technological solutions have sprung up to fill this need.

Many people do their data gathering, calculating, and graphing in Microsoft Excel. Macros can be set up or purchased to assist rapid calculating and graphing. The process behavior charts in this book were produced with CHARTrunner, a commercial program for analyzing data and developing process behavior charts available from PQ Systems (www.pqsystems.com). This program is reasonably priced and powerful. It allows data to be imported from other sources (including Excel and Access) and offers great flexibility in analysis and presentation.

Larger libraries that use integrated programs like Minitab or SAS to manage their data may already have the capabilities required to produce process behavior charts. Applications from iGrafx integrate with Minitab and SAS JMP and offer simulation capability; the iGrafx Process Central package is a comprehensive solution that supports Web-enabled process documentation, version control, and remote access.

MANAGING ONGOING DOCUMENTATION

Each library must decide how to manage the storing and updating of process masters to match its culture and resources. The approach outlined above suggests that this be done centrally by one or two people. We feel that this is the best, most efficient way; it allows the administrator to establish a routine (process) for handling the initial process masters and the changes later made to them.

The library's solution for handling data and other process documentation depends on which software it chooses to do the flowcharts, screens, and key tasks worksheets and how many computers are equipped with the software. If the software is available on the library's intranet or on several computers, the original material can be input by the scribe on the process mastering team. If access is more limited, the library's steering group must ensure that someone enters the data and produces the resulting charts.

Once the data are in the computer, each library must decide how to make them available to others in the library system. If the flowcharts have embedded links to forms, key tasks descriptions, or even remote resources, then the computer screens must be live and not just PDFs.

We recommend that only the process master administrator or process owner be able to make changes to the documents. Otherwise, it is impossible to keep track of which is the current version.

We strongly recommend that process owners manage ongoing gathering and plotting of data. When a standardized and stable process is being worked on for further improvement, it is critical that the process owner and team see what is happening on a daily basis. This happens only if the people in the process do the data work.

ENCOURAGING RELUCTANT EMPLOYEES TO PARTICIPATE

In every organization there are employees who you would prefer were different in some way. Some have not been adequately trained to do their jobs. Some have lived through many initiatives and see this as just one more. Some seem disengaged. Some are simply in the wrong job. You have hundreds of ideas about how to "make them into better employees." The fact is, however, that you have them as they are.

When it comes to continuous improvement, this situation plays out in many ways. Some employees just don't want to participate. Some fear that it is an effort to target them personally or to downsize their department. Some employees are afraid of change in general. Some employees are threatened by any challenge to their domain. Some have never had the opportunity to make their jobs better. Some employees will feel that this whole effort is a waste of their already scarce time. All of these reasons apply to managers as well—negative experiences in the past, fear of change, turf, scarce time. And the reasons could go on and on.

Several approaches work eventually to entice most employees to participate:

Invite rather than tell employees (and managers) to participate on the process mastering and rapid cycle improvement teams. This gives individuals a choice. In the vast majority of cases, those invited will say yes. When the answer is no, they usually have legitimate reasons.

Allow time for employees and managers to observe and get used to the ideas. Often employees who initially choose not to participate are simply waiting to see if the initiative is serious and will continue. When they see that this is an important endeavor, they will participate the next time they are asked.

Offer additional training and coaching. Sometimes employees are reluctant because they do not want to appear stupid. They need safe opportunities to try new tools. They may be willing to participate if the initial effort is viewed as "homework" for their training. For managers, the stakes are even higher, because they might appear incompetent to the people who report to them.

Communicate tangible, exciting results of early team efforts. Communicate even those efforts that have not been completely successful and are stressing the team working on them, as a way of demonstrating that persistence and learning from mistakes are valued by the library.

Empowering employees to standardize and improve their process can result in amazing transformations. Employees flourish in this new culture, where their ideas and experience are valued and respected. Leaders and managers discover their employees' creativity and commitment as well as a new way of working themselves. Pretty soon customers notice improvements and share their delight with others, increasing their perception of the library's value in the community. A story from the Michigan City Public Library shows how process improvement can spread, with the support of leaders.

Spreading Process Improvement at the Michigan City Public Library

Responding to an increased demand for audiovisual materials, lack of space, and a shortage of funds for additional staff, the Michigan City Public Library combined its audiovisual and circulation departments. The newly merged department had twelve staff members, each with a distinct way of doing things. Assistant Director Andy Smith recommended that the staff attend process improvement training as a way to help them develop uniformity throughout the department.

After the first workshop, the four circulation staff members came back with much enthusiasm. Seeing the potential to improve the department, supervisor Sarah Redden gave them her total support. Because of their busy and hectic work schedule, the team had to make the time for meetings to standardize departmental processes. Redden allotted them time to meet weekly for two hours. She also attended the first hour of every meeting, offering comments and answering questions regarding library policy.

To choose which process to work on first, the team compiled a list of more than fifty circulation tasks. They showed the list to everyone in the department and asked them to choose three processes they felt needed the most improvement. Everyone's choices were returned to Redden, who tallied them and made the final decision on what the first process would be.

The four staff members who were attending the workshops worked on the first process. They wanted to get one under their belts and feel comfortable with how the program worked so that they could effectively teach fellow staff members the steps to standardize and improve a process, from beginning to end.

Their first process was "Issue a library card." The group soon realized that this was actually four separate processes, since issuing a card to residents, to reciprocal borrowers, statewide, and to out-of-state residents each had distinct tasks. They began by developing a uniform way to issue a resident library card.

As they were discussing the tasks, they realized that each staff member had a different way of welcoming newly registered patrons and giving them basic information about the library. As their first improvement, they developed a short script, which they called "the spiel," and a handout that they now give to each new patron.

They also realized that patrons who needed to sign up for a card were standing in the same line as those who just wanted to check out materials. Once they got to the desk, it took three or four minutes to fill out the application, complete the registration process, and hear "the spiel"—all of which backed up the line. The group decided to try adding a second station. Now, when a person wants to get a card, a back-up circulation staff member is called and the patron moved out of the check-out line. Thanks to this second improvement, the time for registering for a card has been dramatically reduced, and so has check-out time for the library's other patrons.

After this success, the team moved on to "Issue a reciprocal card." As the process began to take shape, the department as a whole became enthusiastically committed to working together as a team. After gaining hands-on experience developing a process master and making improvements, even skeptics decided that process improvement worked and could be a great tool for creating a more efficient department.

Using the idea of uniformity to guide them, the circulation staff standardized many processes, making sure that every staff member had a solid understanding and acceptance of each process. Given time, they hope to have a complete department process manual that any new employee can pick up, read, and apply successfully.

Since 2004, circulation staff members have taught process mastering and improvement to the shelving department and the reference department. They also discovered that their new way of thinking about continuous improvement carried over into other library services. For example, each year library staff members from several departments went to area elementary schools on registration day. They noticed the registration areas were crowded and appeared somewhat chaotic. Parents were overwhelmed by too much information; all communicated verbally. They began to see the need for a different kind of presentation. After returning to the library, the circulation team members, Redden, and the head of the youth services department met. Using the process techniques they had learned, they developed a packet that showed students and parents how to utilize the full resources and services of the library.

CLOSING WORDS

As we reflect on this book and on our careers, several thoughts come to mind. We believe that work is good. We believe that people are inherently good, and that through their labor they want to help others and leave the world a better place.

We (and others, we are sure) have had times in our careers when we encountered frustration and dissatisfaction with our jobs. We have also had experiences of pure joy while doing our work. In our process improvement work, we have confirmed that several elements lead to the best work experiences—choice, challenge, and collegiality (originally identified in Kohn 1993). The methodology outlined in this book offers these three in abundance.

Most people want *choice* in how they do their work. Process improvement offers choice when employees are invited to participate on a team to standardize a process. At first glance you might think that standardization would be in conflict with choice. In fact it is just the opposite. The workers who do the job, day in and day out, have the choice of how they will do it. They write the process master. Employees have choice in deciding how to measure and which improvements to try.

People are happiest when they are *challenged* and working at their highest mental and physical capabilities. This seems contrary to what many advertisements suggest—that happiness is lounging on the beach with a drink in your hand. The most memorable and rewarding life experiences come when individuals, working with a team, accomplish a major challenge. Improving processes to the point where they surprise and delight customers and their co-workers offers that challenge. To reach that goal, team members learn new ways of working together, create process masters, measure process performance, and design and carry out improvements.

With few exceptions, people like to accomplish things with others. You know what we mean, if, once in your lifetime, you have been privileged to be a member of a team that accomplished great things. *Collegiality* is the essence of process mastering and improvement teams. The approach in this book offers ample opportunities to build and support teams that can accomplish miracles.

For us, the concepts of transforming a library using the systems approach; defining mission, vision, and values; and mastering and improving processes seem simple and straightforward. Our observation of real life reminds us that it isn't easy. We wish you luck. You will be rewarded for embarking on the journey!

NOTE

1. New "lean management" methods incorporate many of the ideas originally described by Deming. See, e.g., Lean Enterprise Institute: http://www.lean.org.

Appendix A | **List of Library Processes**

Broad Processes	Detailed Processes
1. Provide access to Internet-based information	Maintain Internet access in library facilities Update the library website Negotiate database licenses
2. Advise readers	Advise individual readers Make recommended booklists Prepare bibliographies/webliographies
3. Answer phone	Answer phone Transfer calls
4. Answer reference questions	Answer genealogy/local history questions Answer reference questions by IM/chat Answer reference questions by mail Answer reference questions by phone Answer reference questions in person Answer reference questions via e-mail
5. Catalog materials	Conduct original cataloging for local materials Create metadata for archival/special collection items Establish authority records Identify and create metadata Identify corresponding bibliographic record in OCLC Identify local subject headings/call numbers Update bibliographic catalog with Dewey/LC updates
6. Circulate materials	Add delinquent customers to collection agency list Check in materials Check out AV equipment Check out AV materials Check out books Collect fines Collect for damaged or lost items and collection agency fees Empty book drop Identify missing parts of items Refund payments for lost books Release customers from collection agency list

6. Circulate materials (cont.)	Renew materials
	Send delinquent customer list to collection agency
	Send e-mail notices just before due date
	Send overdue notices
	Update record "claims returned"
7. Communicate with customers and stake-holders	Communicate the benefits of the library
	Conduct surveys
	Create promotional materials
	Find lost parents
	Handle complaints
	Handle lost-and-found items
	Make displays
	Participate in community collaborative initiatives
	Participate in community organizations
	Post notice of closure for training and other reasons
	Post notice of public meetings
	Process and distribute incoming faxes
	Process and distribute incoming mail
	Publish annual reports
	Publish newsletters
	Read and respond to e-mail
	Report to funding authorities
	Send faxes
	Send mail
	Send mail and e-mail notices of programs
	Take requests for purchase
	Take requests for reconsideration
8. Create reports	Compile and analyze statistics
	Comply with regulations
	Create portfolios
	Produce board reports
9. Deliver materials	Deliver AV equipment
	Deliver mail to library offices and facilities
	Deliver materials among library facilities
	Deliver materials to other libraries
10. Develop and monitor policies	Develop policies
	Maintain policies
	Monitor policies
11. Evaluate programs and services	Evaluate programs
	Evaluate services

12. Hold board meetings	Create board meeting agendas
	Orient new board members
	Prepare director's reports
	Prepare financial reports
	Prepare special board reports/presentations
	Recruit board members
13. Hold meetings	Create agendas
	Prepare reports/presentations
	Write and distribute minutes
14. Improve processes	Collect and manage data
	Manage process masters
	Write charters
15. Index newspapers	Index newspapers
16. Maintain collection	Clean materials
	Conduct inventory
	Delete items from holdings
	Identify and insure rare items
	Maintain art collection
	Maintain bibliographic database
	Read shelves
	Repair damaged AV materials
	Repair damaged books
	Replace lost and damaged items
	Send items to bindery
	Shift collection
	Transfer materials
	Weed materials
17. Maintain equipment	Install computers and other equipment
	Install new software
	Install software upgrades
	Maintain bookmobiles
	Maintain library-owned vehicles
	Maintain printers—paper, toner, etc.
	Order new computer hardware
	Repair damaged equipment
	Replace damaged computers and other equipment
	Select technology
18. Maintain facilities	Change light bulbs
	Clean bathrooms
	Clean building
	Decorate for holidays
	Inventory equipment
	Maintain grounds

18. Maintain facilities (cont.)	Manage heating/ventilating/air conditioning (HVAC)
	Plan remodeling projects
	Supervise public areas
19. Manage employees	Administer employee benefits (insurance, retirement)
	Administer leave time
	Communicate with employees
	Conduct background checks on candidates
	Counsel employees
	Develop employees
	Evaluate employees
	Handle grievances
	Hire employees
	Interview candidates for positions
	Negotiate union contracts
	Orient new employees
	Post job openings
	Receive job applications
	Schedule employee meetings
	Schedule employees
	Supervise employees
	Train employees
20. Manage funds	Create budget
	Handle cash
	Invest funds
	Make bank deposits
	Manage grants
	Review use of resources
	Select banks for deposit
21. Manage holds	Gather materials on hold
	Place holds
	Pull holds from shelves
	Remove items from hold
22. Manage meeting rooms	Inspect meeting rooms
	Reserve meeting rooms
23. Manage public access to the Internet	Maintain public access computers
	Sign up for computer use
24. Manage reserves	Cancel items on reserve
	Place items on reserve
	Take requests for reserve

25. Manage volunteers	Recognize volunteers Recruit tutors Recruit volunteers Train volunteers Work with Friends of the Library Remove books remaining after Friends book sales
26. Open and close the library	Close the library Close the library in an emergency Collect people counts Open the library
27. Order materials	Negotiate contracts Order and maintain supplies Order books and other materials
28. Pay bills and employees	Pay employees Pay vendors
29. Plan for emergencies	Conduct fire drills Plan for emergencies
30. Plan for the future	Create strategic plans
31. Prepare materials for circulation	Prepare AV materials for circulation Prepare books for circulation Prepare daily newspapers for shelving Prepare periodicals for shelving
32. Present programs	Conduct book discussion groups Conduct computer classes Conduct adult programs Conduct children's programs Conduct young adult programs Place meeting room signs Plan programs Promote programs Set up meeting rooms
33. Provide assistance to customers in library	Answer directional questions Assist at print management stations Assist at self-check stations Assist customers with copiers Assist customers with Internet searches Assist customers with library databases Assist customers with microfilm Assist customers with OPAC Help customers find items

34. Provide outreach	Conduct programs at daycare centers
	Conduct programs at senior centers
	Prepare and deliver deposit collections
	Provide services to homebound customers
35. Provide security	Provide security
36. Raise funds	Accept cash and equity donations
	Conduct annual campaigns
	Maintain donor database
	Plan fund-raising events
	Thank donors
	Write grant proposals
37. Register patrons	Issue new library cards
	Issue out-of-district cards
	Issue out-of-state cards
	Issue reciprocal cards
	Issue replacement library cards
	Issue statewide library cards
	Update patron records
	Verify addresses
38. Request proposals	Request proposals from service providers
39. Select materials	Accept donated materials
	Evaluate donated materials for use in collection
	Evaluate patron requests for purchase
	Renew subscriptions for electronic resources
	Respond to challenged materials
	Select AV materials
	Select new books
	Select new electronic resources
	Select replacement books
	Sort donations
40. Share resources	Fill interlibrary loan requests
	Lend materials among library facilities
	Place interlibrary loan requests with other libraries
	Request materials among library facilities
	Scan articles
	Take interlibrary loan requests
41. Shelve materials	Shelve adult books
	Shelve AV materials
	Shelve children's books
42. Train and educate users	Give tours
	Provide bibliographic instruction

| # Library Process Measures

Note that many of the measurements below can be taken over time. Usually the period should be short—a day, week, or month—so that data can be accumulated in a rapid but systematic way.

Accounting

Accuracy of forecasts

Data entry errors

Actual time compared to estimate

Cost of customer complaints, by type

Actual variance from plan in cost, time or percentage

Number of payments posted incorrectly

Number of incorrect new account documents

Days payable

Days receivable

Number of errors in fund transfers

Number of reports delivered late

Number of vendors

Acquisitions

Cost per item

Percentage of orders received on time

Percentage of orders in which price varies from anticipated

Percentage of unfilled/cancelled orders

Time from order to receipt

Delivery time

Number of internal product complaints, by vendor

Dollar purchases, by type

Percentage of purchases to circulation

Average processing time, by type

Loading/unloading time

Wrong shipments

Percentage of orders shipped most economical way

Percentage of on-time shipments

Number of rejected shipments

Value of rejected shipments

Defects per order, per month

Broken items as percentage of shipment

Time from receipt to shelf

Collection Management

Value of inventory

Percentage growth

Percentage unused

Percentage damaged

Percentage discarded

Value of damaged and discarded materials

Shelving errors detected, by type

Cataloging errors

Processing errors

Cost per use (circulation, gate count, program attendant)

Cost per reference question

Time from return to shelf

Value added time per item

Damaged items

Cost of damaged items

Items declared lost

Overdues

> Number per day
>
> Average time overdue
>
> Percentage overdue
>
> Cost of handling overdues
>
> Percentage returned before overdue notice received
>
> Percentage disputed
>
> Dollars per day

Customer Service

Customer request errors

Variance from customer expectation or specification

Type and number of customer complaints

Gained and lost customer ratios

Complaints from downstream process customers

Percentage of transaction errors

Number of customers served

Percentage satisfied/dissatisfied

Average customer wait time

Number of calls not returned within ___ days

Number of requests not filled

Customers, by type

Usage, by customer type

Human Resources

Recruiting cost per recruit retained

Cost per hire

Number of suggestions for improvement submitted

Number of employees in training

Number of training hours

Training cost per employee

Time to obtain replacement

Orientation cost per employee

Percentage of new employees completing orientation within ___ days of hire

Percentage of correct answers on library training tests

Benefit cost per employee

Number of benefit complaints

Worker's Compensation cost per employee

Turnover rate

Number of grievances

Number of accidents

Percentage of late employees

Average number of late minutes

Time between accidents

Percentage of absent employees

Instruction

Ratio of customers attending to customers using instruction after the session

Instructional sessions per month

Costs per session

Customers per instructor

Information Technology

Minutes of system downtime per month

Programmers per usage

Programming backlog, in days

User entry-response time, in seconds

Desktop equipment downtime, in minutes per month

Number of users per computer technician

Service backlog, by type, in days

Preventive maintenance hours, by type

Program maintenance hours

Number of reports delivered on time

Number of reports actually used

Learning and Growth

Number of new skills implemented

Level of implementation of new skills, innovations

Number of ideas implemented

Dollars or time invested in researching options for the future

Employees promoted

New products/services developed

Value of products/services developed

Number of process improvements

Dollar value of process improvements

Estimated contribution of R&D costs

Number of projects more than ___ days old

Maintenance

Percentage of time doing preventive maintenance

Cycle time from request to completion

Percentage of jobs completed on schedule

Air flow, in cubic feet/minute

Trouble calls per day

Temperature variation

Frequency of unscheduled maintenance or breakdowns

Marketing

Number of customer surveys sent, by type

Percentage of customer surveys returned

Number of competitor's customers interviewed

Time to return calls

Office Support

Number of items misfiled/missing

Percentage of mail returned

Number of data entry errors

Turnaround time

Supplies

    Inventory level

    Cost

    Times that supplies run out

    Value of material no longer used

Outcomes

Customer satisfaction

Percentage of community children reading at grade level by third grade

Invitations to participate in community or school initiatives

Number of individuals who found jobs with library assistance

Homework completed

Adults who learned to read

Objectives of collaborations met

Community skills developed

Dollars raised from all sources for the library

Number of sources of dollars for the library

Number of contributors

Planning

Percent utilization of facilities

Number of employees involved in strategic planning activities

Contributions to key success factors

Scheduling

Percentage of overtime attributed to scheduling

Minutes wasted at beginning and end of shift

Hours of overtime

Timeliness

Number of rings before phone is answered

Percentage of downtime, by machine

Elapsed time for processing insurance claims

Glossary of Process Improvement Terms

Area of opportunity. Range within which data fall. The area of opportunity determines whether counts can be compared directly or must be turned into rates or ratios for purposes of comparison.

Charter. Document that clearly articulates the charge to an individual or group, including authority, limits, and reporting requirements.

Common cause. *See* Variation.

Count. One of two types of measure (the other being measurement).

Customer. Recipient of the outputs of the process or system as a whole. Customers may be internal or external to the organization.

Feedback loop. Communication pathway that ensures that key information is shared by various components within the system. Through such loops, customers provide feedback to the library and the library provides feedback to its suppliers.

Flowchart, deployment. Graphic depiction, organized by individuals or groups responsible for each task, showing each task in a process.

Flowchart, top-down. Graphic depiction of the tasks in a process, from beginning to end.

Input. That which is transformed by a process. Inputs may be tangible (materials, supplies) or intangible (information, perceptions, etc.). Input is delivered to the process by suppliers.

Inspection. Procedure for verifying the quality or completion of a process. Unless used properly, inspection can be considered a waste.

Key process. Process (primary or supporting) that has a significant impact on the ability of a system to produce its outputs, accomplish its mission, and attain its vision. Key processes are particularly relevant to the quality of key outputs to customers.

Key success factor. Action that has the most strategic potential for helping the organization advance its mission, reach its vision, and uphold its values. These are also referred to as goals or objectives in the organization's strategic plan.

Key tasks. Tasks in a process that are important to internal or external customers, suppliers, or the organization.

Lean management. Approach focused on identifying waste in a process or system.

Measure. Objective and subjective numerical data that provide insight into the health of a system, generally focused on quality, time, cost, quantity, and customer satisfaction.

Measurement. One of two types of measure (the other being count).

Mission. Purpose of a system, stated in broad terms.

Moving range. Variation from one data point to another.

Outcome. Value added by a system, measured in terms of customer results.

Output. Transformed input, delivered to customers by a process. Outputs should have added value.

Parking lot. List used by a team to gather and retain ideas that may be valuable in the future.

Plan-Do-Study-Act cycle. Method for rapidly improving processes, developed by Walter Shewhart.

Process. Series of interrelated tasks. A *primary process* is an activity or function that is essential for transforming an input into an output and adds value to the system. A *supporting process* is an activity or function used to improve the efficiency or effectiveness of the primary processes—not essential in the short run, but it can affect the system if neglected in the long run (e.g., maintenance). Supporting processes may be technical (physical activities) or social (related to people).

Process behavior chart. Graphic depiction of process performance, consisting of two graphs, including data points, as well as the average and upper and lower process limits determined through statistical calculations.

Process limit, upper and lower. Statistically defined limits that represent the upper and lower boundaries of natural, or common cause, variation in a stable process.

Process master. Document that describes a process and documents its performance. Process masters include a top-down flowchart, screens of external and internal customers and suppliers, key tasks worksheet, measures, and list of tools/ equipment/supplies/information.

Process mastering. Method of developing a process master in order to reduce variation in and improve a process.

Process owner. Individual responsible for maintaining a process master and ensuring that everyone follows it.

Rapid cycle improvement. Method by which a process improvement team chooses and tests a change in a process, gathers data, and decides, based on the data, whether the change is an improvement. Rapid cycle improvement activity usually follows the Plan-Do-Study-Act cycle.

Run chart. Graphic depiction of process performance, including data points and a line showing the average of the data points. A run chart is the first part of a process behavior chart.

Scatter diagram. Graphic tool used for depicting the importance and condition of processes.

Screen. Graphic tool used to help those studying a process see the relationships between the customer (external and internal) and the process tasks and the supplier and the process tasks.

Special cause. *See* Variation.

Sponsor. Individual who issues a charter.

Steering group. Organization-wide group that oversees process mastering and improvement efforts.

Supplier. Provider of inputs to the process. Suppliers can be internal or external to the organization.

System. Entirety of concern; a series of interrelated processes with a clear aim.

System map. Tool for visualizing the library system, including its mission, vision, values, measures, suppliers, inputs, processes, outputs, customers, and feedback loops.

System name. Description of the system under study.

Tampering. Changing a process because of a common cause variation point of data.

Task. Single action taking place, usually as one piece of a complex process.

Team. Group of employees who are working together to master or improve a process, usually made up of those who work in the process, with the addition of suppliers and customers (external or internal) of the process.

Team leader. Convener of a team.

Team norms. Rules agreed to by the team members for conducting their work and making decisions. Also called group norms or norms.

Values. Principles or qualities held to be important to the organization and everyone in it. Values should guide behavior and be consistent with the organization's mission and vision.

Variation. Inherent differences. In processes, differences from one data point to the next. Common cause variation is the result of natural and predictable differences—points between the calculated process limits in a process behavior chart. Special cause variation is the result of atypical, unusual occurrences—made evident by applying statistical rules in a process behavior chart. Reducing variation is always good.

Vision. Compelling word picture of the future the organization seeks to create. Vision statements should be realistic, credible, attractive, attainable, and challenging.

References

Ackoff, Russell. 1994. *The Democratic Corporation*. New York: Oxford University Press.

Allio, Robert J. 2003. "Russell Ackoff, Iconoclastic Management Authority, Advocates a Systematic Approach to Innovation." *Strategy and Leadership* 31 (3): 19–26.

Barron, Daniel, et al. 2005. *The Economic Impact of Public Libraries on South Carolina*. Columbia: University of South Carolina, College of Mass Communications and Information Studies, School of Library and Information Science. Available at http://www.libsci.sc.edu/SCEIS/home.htm.

Bryce, G. Rex. 1991. "Quality Management Theories and Their Application." *Quality* 30 (January): 15–18.

Cameron, Julie. 1992. *The Artist's Way: A Spiritual Path to Higher Creativity*. New York: Penguin Putnam.

Christensen, Clayton M., Scott D. Anthony, and Erik A. Roth. 2004. *Seeing What's Next: Using the Theories of Innovation to Predict Industry Change*. Boston: Harvard Business School Press.

Csikszentmihalyi, Mihaly. 1990. *Flow*. New York: Harper and Row.

Dalrymple, Prudence Ward. 1990. "User Centered Evaluation of Information Retrieval." Champaign: Allerton Park Institute, University of Illinois Graduate School of Library and Information Science.

Deming, W. Edwards. 1986. *Out of the Crisis*. Cambridge: Massachusetts Institute of Technology, Center for Advanced Engineering Study.

———. 1993. *The New Economics for Industry, Government, Education*. Cambridge: Massachusetts Institute of Technology, Center for Advanced Engineering Study.

———. 2000. *New Economics for Industry, Government, Education*. 2nd ed. Cambridge: MIT Press.

Durrance, Joan C., and Karen E. Fisher, with Marian Bouch Hinton. 2005. *How Libraries and Librarians Help: A Guide to Identifying User-Centered Outcomes*. Chicago: American Library Association.

Everett, Shaunessy. 2006. "Do More, Better, for Less." *Library Journal* 313 (15): 28–31.

Florida Department of State, State Library and Archives of Florida. 2005. *Florida's Public Libraries Build Strong Economies: A Taxpayer Return on Investment Report*. Available at http://dlis.dos.state.fl.us/bld/roi/pdfs/2005_SLAF.ROI.report.pdf.

Galloway, Dianne. 1994. *Mapping Work Processes*. Milwaukee: ASQ Press.

Godfrey, A. Blanton. 2007. "Making Money by Working Smart." July 29. Available at http://www.qualitydigest.com/nov02/columnists/agodfrey.shtml.

Hammer, Michael. 1996. *Beyond Reengineering: How the Process-Centered Organization Is Changing Our Work and Our Lives.* New York: HarperCollins.

Hernon, Peter, and Ellen Altman, 1998. *Assessing Service Quality: Satisfying the Expectations of Library Customers.* Chicago: American Library Association.

Hernon, Peter, and Robert E. Dugan. 2002. *An Action Plan for Outcomes Assessment in Your Library.* Chicago: American Library Association.

Hock, Dee. 1997. "The Birth of the Chaordic Century: Out of Control and Into Order," part 2 of 2. Available at http://www.parshift.com/Speakers/Speak010.htm.

Hoerl, Roger, and Ron Snee. 2002. *Statistical Thinking: Improving Business Performance.* Pacific Grove, CA: Duxbury.

IMLS Institute of Museum and Library Services. 1999. *Outcome-Based Evaluation for IMLS-Funded Projects for Libraries and Museums.* Washington, DC: IMLS.

Joiner, Brian L. 1994. *Fourth Generation Management: The New Business Consciousness.* New York: McGraw-Hill.

Kohn, Alfie. 1993. *Punished by Rewards: The Trouble with Gold Stars, Incentive Plans, A's, Praise, and Other Bribes.* Boston: Houghton Mifflin.

Langley, Gerald J., et al. 1996. *The Improvement Guide: A Practical Approach to Enhancing Organizational Performance.* San Francisco: Jossey-Bass.

Laughlin, Sara, Denise Sisco Shockley, and Ray Wilson. 2003. *The Library's Continuous Improvement Fieldbook: 29 Ready-to-Use Tools.* Chicago: American Library Association.

Lawton, Robin. 2006. "8 Dimensions of Excellence." *Quality Progress,* April.

McGregor, Jena. 2006. "The World's Most Innovative Companies." *Business Week,* April 24.

McNamara, Carter. 1997. "Basic Guide to Outcomes-Based Evaluation for Nonprofit Organizations with Very Limited Resources." Available at http://www.managementhelp.org/evaluatn/outcomes.htm.

Neave, Henry R. 1990. *The Deming Dimension.* Knoxville, TN: SPC Press.

Nelson, Sandra. 2001. *The New Planning for Results: A Streamlined Approach.* Chicago: American Library Association.

Nussbaum, Bruce. 2005. "Get Creative; How to Build Innovative Companies." *Business Week,* August 1.

Ohno, Taiichi. 1988. *Toyota Production System: Beyond Large Scale Production.* Portland, OR: Productivity Press.

O'Neil, Rosanna. 1994. *Total Quality Management in Libraries: A Sourcebook.* Englewood, CO: Libraries Unlimited.

Scherkenbach, William. 1995. "How to Better Implement the Philosophy of Quality." Transformational Leadership Conference, Indianapolis, November 7.

Scholtes, Peter. 1998. *The Leader's Handbook: Making Things Happen, Getting Things Done.* New York: McGraw-Hill.

Scholtes, Peter R., Brian L. Joiner, and Barbara J. Streibel. 1996. *The Team Handbook.* Madison, WI: Joiner Associates.

Seattle Public Library and Foundation. 2005. *The Seattle Public Library Central Library: Economic Benefits Assessment.* 2005. Accessible from http://www.spl.org/default.asp?pageID=branch_central_about&branchID=1.

Shepherdson, Nancy. 2006. "A Sharper Image." *Continental Magazine,* January.

Shewhart, Walter. 1931. *Economic Control of Quality of Manufactured Product.* New York: Van Nostrand.

Snee, Ronald. 2006. "If You're Not Keeping Score, It's Just Practice." *Quality Progress,* May.

Wallace, Linda. 2004. *Libraries, Mission, and Marketing: Writing Mission Statements That Work.* Chicago: American Library Association.

Wheeler, Donald J. 2003. *Making Sense of Data: SPC for the Service Sector.* Knoxville, TN: SPC Press.

Wheeler, Donald J., and David S. Chambers. 1992. *Understanding Statistical Process Control,* 2nd ed. Knoxville, TN: SPC Press.

Wilson, Ray W. and Paul Harsin. 1998. *Process Mastering: How to Establish and Document the Best Known Way to Do a Job.* University Park, IL: Productivity Press.

Index

Sara Laughlin is president of Sara Laughlin & Associates, Inc., a consulting firm specializing in customer-focused, future-oriented planning and evaluation for libraries. Over the past decade, she has worked with Ray Wilson to help libraries develop capacity for improving library processes to meet customer needs and expectations. In 2003 she coauthored *The Library's Continuous Improvement Fieldbook: 29 Ready-to-Use Tools* with Wilson and Denise Sisco Shockley. Laughlin began her career thirty years ago as a reference librarian; since then she has served as a branch manager, consortium director, grant writer, planning specialist, and public library trustee. She occasionally teaches research and evaluation and grant writing at the Indiana University School of Library and Information Science.

Ray W. Wilson is president of Ray Wilson & Associates, consultants in organizational development and operational improvement located in Indianapolis, Indiana. Wilson is a veteran of twenty-eight years as an engineer and executive manager in business and has spent the past ten years as a consultant in continuous improvement to a broad spectrum of clients. He is coauthor of two books: *Process Mastery: How to Establish and Document the Best Known Way to Do a Job* (with Paul Harsin), and *The Library's Continuous Improvement Fieldbook: 29 Ready-to-Use Tools* (with Sara Laughlin and Denise Sisco Shockley). Wilson has BS and MS degrees in agricultural engineering from Pennsylvania State University and is a registered professional engineer. Even though he has a black belt in tae kwon do, he is a really nice guy!